Delta|Academic|Objectives

Writing skills

Louis Rogers

DELTA Publishing
Quince Cottage
Hoe Lane
Peaslake
Surrey GU5 9SW
England

www.deltapublishing.co.uk

First published 2011

Edited by Catriona Watson-Brown
Designed by Caroline Johnston
Photos by Shutterstock (pages 8, 17,
19 arindambanerjee/Shutterstock.com,
23, 31, 33, 34, 42, 50, 55, 58a Anna
Omelchenko/Shutterstock.com, 58b–d,
61, 62 Albo/Shutterstock.com, 65, 67, 74,
79, 80, 82 (right), 85 dutourdumonde/
Shutterstock.com, 89); iStock (pages 44
and 99); CartoonStock (pages 77,
82 (left) and 91)
Cover design by Peter Bushell
Printed in China

ISBN Book 978-1-905085-58-3

Author acknowledgements

I would like to thank various people for their help in the development of this book. In particular, I would like to thank Emma Kuhles, Nashwa Nashaat, Diane Schmitt and Liz Wilding for their valuable feedback. I would also like to thank Val Baker, Dawn Clarke, Prue Griffiths and Clare Nukui for the valuable discussions and input. For taking the time to meet with me and discuss the concept, I would like to thank Philip Lodge, Mary Mayall, Asmaa Awad, Dr Siddig and William Vize. Thank you to the many people at DELTA Publishing for their help the development of this book. For all the editorial support and feedback, I would like to thank Catriona Watson-Brown. For the fantastic design work, Caroline Johnston. From developing the concept to helping push it forward to the product it is, I would like to thank Nick Boisseau and Chris Hartley. I would also especially like to thank my wife, Cathy Rogers, for all her support and patience during the writing.

Text acknowledgements

We are grateful to the following for permission to reproduce copyright material:

Cambridge University Press for extracts from *Testing for Language Teachers*, by Arthur Hughes, Cambridge University Press, 2003, pp.1, 5, copyright © Cambridge University Press; Pearson Education Limited for extracts from *Management: An Introduction*, 4th edition, by David Boddy, 2008, pp.52, 494, 496, 500, 503, 504, copyright © Pearson Education Limited; Taylor & Francis Books for extracts from *Redesigning English: new texts new identities* by David Graddol, Sharon Goodman and Theresa Lillis, Routledge, 2007, pp.256, 258, 253, copyright © Taylor & Francis Books; The British Council and David Graddol for the graphs 'Changing demography of internet users by first language' published in *English Next* by David Graddol, 2006, p.44, www.britishcouncil.org, reproduced with permission; Miniwatts Marketing Group for statistics from 'The changing demography of Internet users by first language' 2005, www.worldinternetstats.com, copyright © 2000–2011, Miniwatts Marketing Group. All rights reserved; The Home Office for the figure 'Crime trends in England and Wales' 1982–2004, as published in 'Violent crime "rise" sparks row' by the BBC, 21 April 2005, http://news.bbc.co.uk/1/hi/uk_politics/vote_2005/frontpage/ 4467569.stm, 21 April 2005, © Crown Copyright, 2011; Polity Press for extracts from *Sociology* by Anthony Giddens, 2006, pp.811–812, copyright © Polity Press; The McGraw-Hill Companies for extracts from *International Marketing*, 12th edition, by Philip R. Cateora and John L. Graham, 2005, pp.99, 102, 103, 114, copyright © The McGraw-Hill Companies; U.S. Energy Information Administration for the figure 'Shares of world energy consumption in the USA, China and India 1990–2035', Figure 14, p.2 from *World Energy Demand and Economic Outlook*, http://www.eia.gov/oiaf/ieo/pdf/world.pdf. Source: U.S. Energy Information Administration, 2010; United Nations for the graph 'World population growth, 1950–2050', United Nations Population Division *World Population Prospects, The 2008 Revision*, http://www.prb.org/Educators/TeachersGuides/HumanPopulation/PopulationGrowth.aspx, copyright © United Nations; and Government Office for Science for a graph from Foresight: *Tackling Obesities: Future Choices – Project Report*, Government Office for Science, 2007.

In some instances, we have been unable to trace the owners of copyright material and we would appreciate any information that would enable us to do so.

Contents

evaluating writing	critical thinking	language focus
Stages for evaluating and editing work	Formulating research questions	1 Key aspects of academic writing 2 Academic register
Editing grammar	Interpreting and evaluating data	The Academic Word List
Spelling and punctuation	Distinguishing fact from opinion	1 Using past and present tenses 2 Word formation
Self-editing	Producing logical arguments – reasons and conclusions	Word formation
Hedging and academic language	Supporting evidence and examples	1 Using modals and hedging language 2 Alternative and counter-arguments

evaluating critical thinking in writing		language focus
Strength and logic of argument		1 Using synonyms and pronoun referents 2 Using connecting language
Paragraph logic		Using noun collocations
Evaluating solutions		1 Verb collocations 2 Active and passive
Relevance and support		Comparing and contrasting
Overgeneralizations		1 Cause and effect 2 Describing trends

Introduction

Understanding the expectations of academic writing is a challenge for all students, not just those learning English as a second language. The structure, style and use of sources are just a few of the expectations that make academic writing different from other genres. This book forms part of the *Delta Academic Objectives* series that will help you to adapt to the challenges of studying academically in the English language.

The texts

There are only brief texts within this book to practise different sub-skills. However, there are additional texts online at www.deltapublishing.co.uk/resources, and there is a strong thematic link with the *Reading skills* book in this series. The topics cover a wide range of subject areas, including some of the most commonly found disciplines in academic study. You do not have to be a specialist in the field to study these texts, as the topics are both academic and common to everyday life.

Aims

This book aims to prepare you for the challenges of writing academically. It does this by covering five main areas.

- **Essay structure and organization**

  A well-structured essay has many stages to it, from the moment you read the essay question to revising your final draft. It is important to think about questions such as:
  - What exactly does this essay question require?
  - How can my ideas be best organized?
  - How can I structure each paragraph effectively?
  - What are the differences between some of the main essay types?

- **Critical thinking**

  One of the key challenges you will face when writing is to engage critically with the academic community. This involves not simply accepting ideas that are written but learning to constantly challenge and question the ideas of others. You need to ask yourself questions such as:
  - Is my argument logical?
  - What evidence is there, and how have I used it?
  - What weaknesses are there in the argument?
  - Am I presenting the argument objectively?

- **Using the text**

  In general English, it is quite common to write without any need to support your opinion. However, in academic writing, you will, in most cases, be expected to strengthen and support your opinion using your research. It can help to think about points such as:
  - Which part of the text best supports my opinion?
  - How can I put this into my own words?
  - How can I show this is another person's idea?
  - How can I include it in my essay?'

  This skill is also practised further in the companion book, *Delta Academic Objectives: Reading skills*.

- **Language focus**

  By developing your knowledge of lexis typical of academic texts, you will not only be able to understand a wider range of texts but also start to transfer this knowledge into your writing. The exercises in this section will help you to develop these skills and think about points such as:
  - What vocabulary should I learn?
  - Should I learn the word by itself or a whole phrase?
  - How does this vocabulary connect ideas in the text?

  These skills are also practised further in the companion book, *Delta Academic Objectives: Reading skills.*

- **Evaluating writing**

  You are likely to receive much feedback from your English teachers or the teachers from your discipline at undergraduate or postgraduate study. It is important that you act upon all feedback you receive and use it to improve future writing. This section will help you to develop these skills and think about points such as:
  - How accurate is my use of English?
  - How well organized are my ideas?
  - Have I included sources effectively?
  - Have I demonstrated my understanding of the topic?
  - Where necessary, have I been critical in my writing in an effective way?

  In the second half of the book, the *Critical thinking* and *Evaluating writing* sections merge so you can start to evaluate aspects of critical thinking in writing.

At the end of the book, there are two review checklists, which you can use on a wide range of essays.

How to use this book

There are 12 units in this book: ten of these each cover a different theme, and the other two (Units 6 and 12) are revision units, giving you the chance to review what you have learned. The main units do not have to be studied in order – you can use the contents list on pages 4 and 5 to select the areas or topics that you feel are of most use or interest to you. However, it is advisable to study whole units and not just particular sections, as the exercises in the different sections are often interrelated. The revision units relate to the skills areas covered in the preceding five units, so it is a good idea to ensure that you have done all five before tackling the revision exercises.

The Academic Word List (AWL)

In line with the theme of language development, the AWL is also a feature of this book (see Unit 2 for more details). At the end of the book are ten pages (one for each sub-list of the AWL) with exercises to test some of the vocabulary in the sub-lists. These can be done at any time and subsequently revisited to check what you have remembered. The ten sub-lists also appear at the end of the book for easy reference.

> There is a substantial bank of texts for further practice online at
> www.deltapublishing.co.uk/resources.

1 Education

- Understanding question words
- Formulating research questions
- Writing notes and summaries
- Introduction to key aspects of academic writing and register
- Evaluating and editing work

Topic focus

1 **Look at the images above. Can you put them in order? If so, why did you choose that order?**

2 **Discuss these questions with partner.**

　1 What is the main aim of studying?

　2 What reasons are there for choosing particular subjects?

　3 Is it important to assess knowledge?

　4 How can knowledge be best assessed?

　5 How do you personally prefer to be assessed?

3 **Look at these words. Work with a partner to divide them into two groups. Think about both meaning and/or form, e.g. which are verbs and which are nouns?**

analyze　assessment　compare　coursework　define　discuss　education
grades　marks　outline　school　a study　summarize　a test　university

4 a **Work with another pair. Compare how you divided the words in Exercise 3.**

　b **Try to give a title to the other pair's lists.**

Essay structure and organization: understanding question words

1 a Look at these two essay questions and underline the difference in them. How does this one difference change focus of the question?

1 Describe the testing system in American high schools.

2 Evaluate the testing system in American high schools.

> ℹ️ You saw some of these words in the *Topic focus* section. These types of words are often called *instruction words*; they indicate how you should deal with the topic.

b Brainstorm other instruction words with a partner.

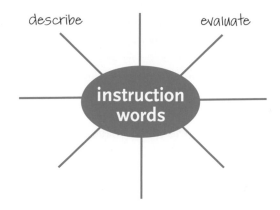

2 Work with a partner. Match the instruction words (1–6) to their definitions (a–f). Then do the same for 7–12 and g–l.

1 analyze	**a** to examine or judge two or more things in order to show how they are similar to or different from each other
2 compare	
3 define	**b** to talk or write about something in detail and consider different ideas and opinions about it
4 discuss	
5 describe	**c** to explain the exact meaning of a word or idea
6 evaluate	**d** to say what someone or something is like by giving details about them
	e to judge how good, useful or successful something is
	f to examine something in detail

7 explain	**g** to look at something carefully and thoroughly
8 examine	**h** to give a good and acceptable reason for something
9 outline	**i** to give a reason for something
10 illustrate	**j** to state how much an idea is or isn't true
11 justify	**k** to make the meaning clear by giving examples
12 to what extent	**l** the main ideas or facts about something, without the details

> ℹ️ Question words will often tell you whether the essay type is evaluative, argument, analytical or descriptive.

3 Complete the descriptions below of four main essay types with the words in the box.

| argument | analytical | descriptive | evaluative |

1 An _____ essay uses facts to support personal opinion. It judges and compares a range of things/ideas using examples and explanations, resulting in your conclusion.

2 An _____ essay uses reasons and evidence to build a case for or against an idea.

3 An _____ essay is a piece of writing in which you must look in detail at a text, theory or ideas.

4 Arguing, interpreting and evaluating are not key to _____ essays. Explaining a process or sequence of events is.

4 Which of these essay questions ask for a more descriptive approach, and which for a more evaluative approach?

a   Define the following educational terms:
   ● summative assessment
   ● formative assessment.

b   Examine the strengths and weaknesses of the British education system.

c   Discuss the effectiveness of tests as a method of assessment.

d   Assessment via coursework is biased towards girls. To what extent do you agree with this statement?

> *i* It is important that the introduction to an essay is clearly linked to the title. A reader should not need to know the essay question to be able to understand your purpose for writing.

5 a Look at these sentences and underline the instruction word in each one.

1 This essay will compare the methods of testing and coursework assessment used in British schools.

2 This essay will outline the methods of testing and coursework assessment used in British schools.

3 This essay will evaluate the methods of testing and coursework assessment used in British schools.

b The above sentences all come from essay introductions. How might these three essays be different?

Study tip
It is always important to break a question into parts to clearly understand what is expected of you. Otherwise there is a greater risk of including information that is not relevant to the task.

Critical thinking: formulating research questions

1 Look at these essay questions (a–c) and answer the questions below (1–3).

a   Analyze the British education system.

b   Analyze the changes in the British education system.

c   Analyze the changes in the British education system under the current government.

> **Study tip**
> After analyzing what an essay question expects you to do, it is important to plan your research. One step is to think about what sub-questions need to be asked in order to answer the question.

   1 How many parts are there to each question?

   2 Imagine you have to write a 1,000-word essay on one of the above. Which essay do you think would be easier to write, and why?

   3 What different information would you need to find for each question?

2 Work with a partner and answer these questions about the essay question below.

   1 What different viewpoints might there be on the opinion expressed in the question?

   2 Do you agree or disagree with the opinion?

   3 What questions would you need to ask to find evidence to prove or disprove it?
Example: When do people normally start school?

Four years old is too young to start education. Discuss.

3 Compare your questions from Exercise 2 with those below. Do you agree that these are the right questions that need to be asked? Why? / Why not?

   1 What different ages do people start school?

   2 What is the best method of education?

   3 Do any school systems start at the age of four? How successful are these systems in comparison to systems where students start later?

   4 What would be the impact of changing the system, e.g. economic, political, social?

   5 Should students be tested at a young age?

   6 What should four-year-olds study?

4 a Look at this essay question. What further research questions can you add to the list below?

The Internet has encouraged plagiarism and should be banned for academic research. To what extent do you agree with this statement?

- Is copying more common today?
- Does the Internet encourage copying?
- What other sources could be used?

b Compare your questions with a partner.

5 Choose one of the four essay questions from Exercise 4 on page 10 and think of research questions you need to ask in order to answer it.

Using sources: writing notes and summaries

1 Discuss with a partner what you understand by each of these terms.

1 summarizing

2 note-taking

3 paraphrasing

2 Match these terms (1–3) to the correct definitions (a–c).

1 notes

2 summarize

3 paraphrase

a to express in a shorter, clearer or different way what someone has said or written

b information that a student writes down from a book, seminar, etc.

c to make a short statement giving only the main information and not the details

> This unit will focus on summary-writing and note-taking. For further information on paraphrasing, see Unit 4.

3 Discuss these questions with a partner.

1 Why do we take notes and summarize?

2 What are good note-taking and summarizing skills?

4 a Work with a partner. What do you think is the difference between active note-taking and passive note-taking?

b Divide these activities into active and passive note-taking styles. What would be the benefits of the more active styles?

1 underlining words

2 copying lots of direct quotes

3 thinking about your research aims before you start

4 cutting and pasting from the Web

5 recording direct quotes only when the exact words are important

6 producing notes on everything you read

7 not evaluating and criticizing sources, simply accepting them as useful evidence

8 looking for answers to research questions

9 noting mainly in your own words

5 a Look at the paragraph below and decide which of these three sentences best summarizes the main idea.

a Assessment is important in education.

b Assessment is important in education to test students' progress.

c Assessment is important to maintain standards in education.

Assessment is vital to any teaching and learning. The minimum that students and teachers need to know is that a required standard has been reached for particular awards. More importantly, without adequate information about what has or has not been learned, whether subject knowledge or skills, students cannot progress, teachers cannot assess their own teaching, and institutions cannot have confidence in the awards they offer.

b **Compare your answer with a partner. If you have chosen different sentences, explain your choice.**

6 a **Spend one or two minutes studying this paragraph. Then close your book and write a one-sentence summary without looking back at the paragraph.**

> Many language teachers harbour a deep mistrust of tests and of testers. The starting point for this book is the admission that this mistrust is frequently well founded. It cannot be denied that a great deal of language testing is of very poor quality. Too often, language tests have a harmful effect on teaching and learning, and fail to measure accurately whatever it is they are intended to measure.

b **Compare your sentence with a partner. Did you select the same main ideas?**

7 a **Read the two paragraphs below, then make notes in this table of the main points relating to formative and summative assessment.**

formative assessment	summative assessment

Assessment is formative when teachers use it to check on the progress of their students, to see how far they have mastered what they should have learned, and then use this information to modify their future teaching plans. Such assessment can also be the basis for feedback to the students. Informal tests or quizzes may have a part to play in formative assessment, but so will simple observation (of performance on learning tasks, for example) and the study of portfolios that students have made of their work. Students themselves may be encouraged to carry out self-assessment in order to monitor their progress, and then modify their own learning objectives.

Summative assessment is used at, say, the end of the term, semester or year in order to measure what has been achieved by both groups and individuals. Here, for the reasons given in the previous section, formal tests are usually called for. However, the results of such tests should not be looked at in isolation. A complete view of what has been achieved should include information from as many sources as possible. In an ideal world, the different pieces of information from all sources, including formal tests, should be consistent with each other. If they are not, the possible sources of these discrepancies need to be investigated.

b **Keep your notes for a week. Then, without looking back at the text, write a brief summary.**

Study tip
Notes can often be used a long time after they were written, so it is important that they make sense in the future.

 When making notes and summaries for later use in writing an essay, it is important to include certain information for references and bibliographies.

8 a **Which of these pieces of information do you think you need for a bibliography or reference?**

1 author's surname and initial
2 chapter title of all books used
3 full address of the publisher
4 full name of the author
5 name of the publisher
6 page of all references
7 page of direct quotes only
8 place of publication
9 title of the book
10 year of publication
11 year of reprint

b **Compare your answers with a partner.**

Language focus 1: key aspects of academic writing

1 Discuss these questions with a partner.

   1 What makes academic writing different from other forms of writing?

   2 What do you want to improve about your writing?

2 Answer these questions individually, then discuss your answers with a partner.

   1 Write down the first 12 verbs that you can think of. How common do you think these verbs are in academic writing?

   2 The present tense is the most common tense in academic writing. True or false?

   3 A wide range of grammatical tenses are used in academic writing. True or false?

   4 Are nouns or verbs more common in academic writing?

   5 How common do you think contractions (for example *it's*) are in academic writing?

   6 What do you understand by the term *noun phrase*?

   7 What is a relative clause? How is it commonly used?

   8 The passive is commonly used in academic writing. Why do you think this is?

   9 Pronouns are a common feature of academic writing. True or false?

3 Consider your answers to the questions in Exercise 2. Have they changed your answers to Exercise 1?

Language focus 2: academic register

1 Look at these two texts. Which is from an academic text, and which is from a blog? What features helped you to make your choice? Look at *Language focus 1* for ideas.

Text A

Assessment is vital to any teaching and learning. The minimum that students and teachers need to know is that a required standard has been reached for particular awards. More importantly, without adequate information about what has or has not been learned, whether subject knowledge or skills, students cannot progress, teachers cannot assess their own teaching, and institutions cannot have confidence in the awards they offer.

Text B

It's not that long since I took my SATs, but I have a clear memory of everyone I ever spoke to saying 'don't worry, they don't mean anything'. I guess they were trying to be reassuring and make sure I didn't worry, but as a result, I didn't try and neither did anyone else. All SATs do and have ever done is stress out kids, for the sake of judging schools – it doesn't teach the kids anything, just how to pass exams – why not get kids actually out there and actually learning the actual skills they're going to need in the real world?

2 Match these non-academic features (1–6) to the sentences they appear in (a–e). Some sentences can relate to more than one feature.

   1 personal

   2 subjective

   3 assertive

   4 contractions

   5 active voice

   6 colloquial vocabulary

   a It could be argued that the consequences haven't been fully considered.

   b I interviewed 12 people on the topic of school starting age.

   c Clearly, without doubt, starting school at four is too young.

   d Kids need to develop further in the home environment before entering the school system.

   e I believe that a balance of coursework and test assessment provides the most accurate view of a student's ability.

3 Rewrite the sentences in Exercise 2 so that they are more academic in style.

Evaluating writing: stages for evaluating and editing work

 This book looks at two main areas to edit: language and critical thinking. It also covers self-editing, responding to peer feedback and teacher feedback. Editing your work and responding to feedback is key in both the learning process and improving the standard of work you submit. Being critical of your own work and responding positively to criticism from others will help improve your writing.

Self-editing 1 a **Match these topics for this section in the book (1–9) to their explanations (a–i).**

1 editing grammar errors

2 overgeneralizations

3 paragraph logic

4 strength and logic of argument

5 spelling and punctuation

6 hedging and academic style

7 range of structures

8 evaluating solutions

9 relevance and support

a using cautious language and a formal style of writing

b correcting tenses, word formation, subject–verb agreement, missing words, etc.

c checking that all information is directly related to the topic

d checking that all information refers back to the question and any opinion stated in the introduction

e checking that claims and statements are not made about more people or a larger situation than the data support

f checking that all information in one part of the essay follows logically from a main topic and supports this idea

g checking for a variety of forms and avoiding always using the same structure

h checking for the correct use of commas, full stops, capital letters, etc. and checking spelling

i looking at the strengths and weaknesses suggested in the solving of a problem

b **Divide the topics 1–9 above into two groups: *language* and *critical thinking*.**

c **Language and critical thinking are not often dealt with at the same time. Why do you think this is?**

Peer feedback 2 a **Work with a partner. In what ways do you think your work could benefit from peer feedback?**

b **Which of these statements represent ways in which peer feedback could benefit you?**

1 It could save you time doing research, as you could use your partner's work.

2 An essay is written for a reader, so it is important someone reads it before submitting it.

3 Something that is clear to you might not be clear to someone else.

4 You could cut and paste ideas from each other's work to save time.

5 It can give you a different perspective on the same issue.

6 You can find out what is interesting and works well, as well as the negative parts.

> **Study tip**
> As well as editing and evaluating your own work, working with a peer to provide feedback can be a valuable way of improving your work.

3 Read these comments provided as feedback. Which do you think are most useful, and why?

1 A lot of the essay wasn't clear, and I didn't understand it.

2 You have some interesting ideas, but there isn't enough support.

3 There are a lot of grammar mistakes.

4 In paragraph 2, the third and fourth sentences are not related to the main topic.

5 The introduction is very general and does not give me a clear idea of your opinion.

6 I like the essay a lot. It's very interesting.

> ℹ Feedback you provide to a partner should be clear and detailed. It is important that the feedback gives the writer something specific to improve.

Teacher feedback **4 a Look at these comments made by different teachers. Write what you understand by each one.**

1 You have made a number of word-formation errors.

2 More critical analysis needed.

3 You have only described the theory and not provided any evaluation.

4 You have not supported your opinions with research.

5 Your essay is based solely on personal opinion and is very subjective.

6 Your paragraphs are not clearly structured and have multiple topics in each.

b Compare your answers with a partner.

> ℹ If you do not understand your teacher's feedback, make sure you ask. It is important you learn from feedback and apply it in future writing.

Unit extension

1 Find five essay questions related to your future area of study. For each one:

1 identify the key question word and analyze each question;

2 write a brief description of what the essay question is expecting you to do.

2 Find a longer text related to an essay question in this unit or in your field of study.

1 Practise the summary-writing and active note-taking skills described in this unit.

2 Give your text and summary to a partner. Does your partner agree with your summary?

2 Leadership

Aims

- Developing and organizing ideas
- Introduction to the Academic Word List
- Interpreting and evaluating data
- Writing definitions
- Editing grammar

Topic focus

Excellent work, well done!

1 a **Work with a partner. Look at the pictures above. Which one do you think would make you happiest?**

b **Imagine your future job. List five things that would make you happy about this job.**

Example: status

2 a **Look at these pairs of ideas. Circle the one in each pair you think is more motivating.**

1 money / praise

2 promotion / relationship with peers

3 achievement / status

4 security / responsibility

5 relationship with supervisor / work itself

b **Compare your answers with a partner.**

3 **Look at these two words and discuss the questions below with a partner.**

> motivation   leadership

1 How do you think they are connected?

2 How do you think a leader can best motivate others?

3 Think of a leader you know. How do they motivate others?

Essay structure and organization: developing and organizing ideas

1 Look at this essay question and discuss the questions below.

> Allowing people to be creative and to make their own decisions are the most effective tools for motivating employees. Discuss.

1 Are all employees motivated by creativity?
2 Are all employees motivated by being able to make their own decisions?
3 What other factors motivate people?

2 a Use the essay question and discussion questions in Unit 1 to write down all your ideas related to the topic.

b Compare your ideas with a partner.

c Form a group of four and write one complete list of ideas.

 The steps in Exercises 1 and 2 are often called *brainstorming*. They are important stages in forming first ideas and can help with research and essay structure.

3 Look at this mind map showing how ideas on this topic could be connected, then answer the questions below.

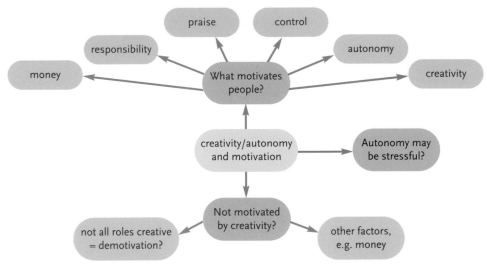

1 How has this person connected their ideas?
2 How do you think this person is planning to organize their essay?

 Planning research questions is key to limiting your research time and to making your reading focused. It can also help to organize your writing.

4 a What topics will the author of the mind map in Exercise 3 need to find evidence to support?

b Write five possible research questions this person could ask.
  Example: Is money key to motivation?

c Compare your answers to Exercises 4a and 4b with a partner.

Language focus: the Academic Word List

 The Academic Word List (AWL) is a list of just under 600 words that are commonly found in academic texts. Ten per cent of an average academic text is made up of words from the AWL. Learning these words will clearly help you to understand an academic text, but using them will also help to formalize your own writing, as they are one of the features of a text that make it sound more academic in style.

1 **Look at these pairs of examples. For each pair, use the context to work out the meaning of the word in bold and write a definition of it.**

1 Using computer programs, filing, emailing and sending letters are some of the **administration** tasks required for the role.

2 Governmental work can be quite bureaucratic and contain a lot of form-filling. Many people often complain about this **administration** side to their job.

administration: _____

3 **Contemporary** leadership often involves allowing people more power in the decision-making process. In the past, many decisions were made at the top of a company, with few people involved.

4 Many **contemporary** practices in today's companies are still influenced by theories developed over 50 years ago.

contemporary: _____

5 There are many **experts** in the field of motivation, but perhaps the best known is Maslow and his theory of the hierarchy of needs.

6 In large companies, people often have very specific and clearly defined roles, which enables them to become **experts** in this area.

expert: _____

7 In some countries, there is a clear power distance between staff and managers, which results in quite a **hierarchy**, with many clearly defined levels of seniority

8 A hierarchy with many levels can make decision-making quite slow. Many companies have moved to a flatter **hierarchy** to both save costs and make decision-making quicker.

hierarchy: _____

9 Charities such as Oxfam often take the lead in providing **aid** to areas of the world that have suffered from a crisis such as an earthquake.

10 Financial **aid** is provide to unemployed people in the UK.

aid: _____

2 Complete each of the sentences below using the word in the box that is synonymous with the words in brackets.

formulation	focus	principle	resources	underlying	vision

1 The _____ of the marketing strategy was key to the successful launch of the product. (*creation, putting together, development*)

2 Steve Jobs has a very clear _____ for his product concepts and the design and use of technology. (*idea, image, mental picture*)

3 The _____ behind many theories of leadership is to make people perform to a higher level. (*rule, theory, notion*)

4 The _____ of the presentation was the application of Maslow's theory to a group of workers in a small IT company. (*centre, heart, hub*)

5 The development of renewable sources of energy has increased in recent years due to people's concerns that oil _____ are running out. (*supply, store, reserve*)

6 The _____ principle of the theory is that factors such as money only provide short-term motivation. (*basic, main, principle*)

3 Match each set of words (1–6) to the words on the right (a–f) to form collocations. Say whether the words in 1–6 go before or after their collocates.

1 foreign / legal / humanitarian   **a** underlying

2 music / art / dance   **b** principle

3 medical / financial / technical   **c** resources

4 cause / principle / problem   **d** expert

5 basic / fundamental / guiding   **e** contemporary

6 financial / limited / human   **f** aid

4 Complete these sentences with collocations from Exercise 3.

1 The _____ department of a company deals with issues such as staff training and the hiring and firing of employees.

2 The _____ of Theory X and Theory Y is the earlier motivational hierarchy developed by Maslow.

3 People in the UK on a low income are entitled to _____ if they do not have the money to pay for a lawyer or solicitor.

4 _____ can work in a wide range of fields from forensics to plastic surgery.

5 The _____ was not so much the change but the manner in which the changes were implemented.

6 _____ causes much discussion and debate, partly because not everybody believes you need to be talented to produce it.

5 For each of the words in this section, produce a vocabulary card like this one.

Pronunciation	**Synonyms**
/fɔːmjʊˈleɪʃən/	creation, putting together, development
Word family	**Example sentence**
noun: *formulation*	*The **formulation** of the plan was key to the final outcome.*
verb: *formulate*	
adjective: –	**Collocations**
adverb: –	*formulation of*

Critical thinking: interpreting and evaluating data

 Research can produce data that are very varied and also use a variety of research methods. It is important whenever you read a claim to consider the research methods used, the type and amount of data collected and the claims made on the basis of the research.

1 **Read the description of a study below and answer these questions.**

 1 What is the possible limitation of this study?

 2 How transferable do you think the ideas might be to other studies?

 3 How could any claims made by this study be made stronger?

> **Fayol's principles of management**
> Throughout Fayol's career, he kept detailed diaries and notes about his management experiences, and his reflections on these formed the basis of his work after retirement. Fayol credited his success as a manager to the methods he used, not to his personal qualities. He believed that managers should use certain principles in performing their functions.

2 **Read the description of another study below and answer these questions.**

 1 What else do you need to know to be able to judge McGregor's claims?

 2 What do you need to know about Maslow's study to be able to accept McGregor's claims?

 3 What are the strengths and weaknesses of basing a theory on another theory?

> ## McGregor's theories of motivation
>
> McGregor presented two sets of assumptions underlying management practice: Theory X, which he called the traditional view of direction and control, and Theory Y, which suggests that people accept responsibility, and apply imagination, ingenuity and creativity to organizational problems. McGregor's work was based on Maslow's hierarchy of needs. He grouped Maslow's hierarchy into 'lower order' (Theory X) needs and 'higher order' (Theory Y) needs.

3 **Read the description of a third study below and answer these questions.**

 1 What possible weaknesses are there in the study?

 2 How could the study have been strengthened?

> ### Herzberg's theory of motivation
>
> While Maslow and McClelland focused on individual differences in motivation, Herzberg (1959) related motivation to the nature of a person's work. He developed his theory following interviews with 200 engineers and accountants about their experience of work.

4 a **Work with a partner and compare your answers to Exercises 1–3.**

 b **On the basis of what you know about each piece of research, which do you think is potentially the strongest study?**

 c **Summarize your criticism of each theory and present your summaries to another pair.**

5 a Read the criticisms below of the studies in Exercises 1–3. Do they match your own criticisms from Exercise 4?

b Underline language used to make the criticism. The first one has been done.

The study was therefore not based on the typical worker, since accountants and engineers would, of course, have been well above the national average for wages and working conditions. (Tum, Norton, Wright, 2006)

There are two common general criticisms of Herzberg's theory. One is that the theory has only limited application to 'manual' workers. (Mullins, 2007)

Some management experts have opposed the thoughts of Fayol, arguing that these principles are based on limited study. (Singla, 2009)

After reviewing 22 studies, Wabha Bridwell concludes 'review shows that Maslow's theory has received little clear or consistent support [...] some of the propositions are totally rejected, while others receive mixed and unquestionable support at best. (Sudan and Kumar, 2004)

McGregor, like Maslow before him, dealt in unwarranted generalizations about the inherent nature of employees. (Duncan, 1982)

6 a Complete the sentences below using the words and expressions in the box.

advanced thoughts against	based on limited study	in isolation
limited application	little clear and consistent support	opposed
too narrow	unwarranted generalizations	

1 Hofstede's theory describes culture in terms of only five aspects. Many people have criticized this for being a _____ focus.

2 A study based solely on personal experience is likely to have _____ to other contexts.

3 Since the idea was first proposed, there has been _____ to show that the theory is actually true.

4 Many studies in the field of management have been hindered by the fact that they are _____ and therefore lack transferability to differing contexts.

5 Whilst Belbin's theory is widely used, many have _____ the idea that the perfect team exists.

6 New theories often develop or evolve when an individual or group of individuals is _____ to an existing idea.

7 The concept makes _____ about wider groups than the study was originally based.

8 The concept of one motivating factor operating _____ is unlikely, as many different points come together to motivate a person.

b Choose three of the expressions from above to write sentences about the studies in Exercises 1–3. Use the ideas you generated in Exercise 4 to help you.

c Exchange sentences with a partner. Have they used the expressions correctly?

Using sources: writing definitions

1 a Answer these questions.

    1 Do you think there is a difference between a leader and a manager?

    2 What is the definition of *manager*?

    3 If you believe a leader is different to a manager, write a definition of *leader*.

b Compare your definitions with a partner.

> Two common methods of defining terms or concepts in academic writing are the use of relative clauses and nouns followed by prepositional phrases.

2 a Which of these definitions best reflects your own opinion?

    1 Drucker (1999) defines leadership as 'the lifting of people's vision to higher sights, the raising of their performance to a higher standard, the building of their personality beyond its normal limitations'.

    2 Managers and leaders often influence people who are equally powerful. (Boddy, 2008)

    3 A manager is someone who gets things done with the aid of people and other resources. (Boddy, 2008)

    4 Leadership refers to the process of influencing the activities of others toward high levels of goals setting and achievement. (Boddy, 2008)

b Which two definitions include relative clauses?

c Circle the nouns and underline the prepositional phrases that follow them in the definitions above. The first one has been done for you.

3 a Look at these two definitions of *strategy*. The first has key parts underlined. Underline the same features in the second definition.

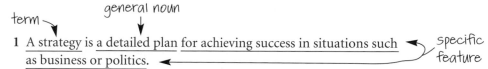

    term   *general noun*   *specific feature*

    1 A strategy is a detailed plan for achieving success in situations such as business or politics.

    2 A strategy is a detailed plan which aims to achieve success in situations such as business or politics.

b Which pattern ('preposition + noun/verb' or relative clause) do you think is more common in academic writing?

> Noun phrases are common in academic writing because it is possible to include a lot of information in the phrase. Being concise is an important skill to learn in academic writing.

4 Complete each of the sentences below using one word or expression from Box A and one from Box B.

A

> a desired future   a guideline   a person
>
> a series   a social arrangement

B

> an activity   achieving   arranging   related   things done

1 A goal is _____ for _____ or organizational unit.

2 A manager is _____ who gets _____ with the aid of other people.

3 An organization is _____ for _____ controlled performance towards common goals.

4 A procedure is _____ of _____ steps to deal with a problem.

5 A hierarchy is _____ for _____ people or things into an order of importance.

5 a Choose two terms related to the concepts of leadership, management and motivation and write a definition for each one.

b Exchange definitions with a partner. Are your partner's clear?

Evaluating writing: editing grammar

 The exercises in this section look at some typical grammatical mistakes that occur in writing. After correcting these mistakes, pay attention to your own writing in the same way.

1 Correct the mistakes with verb forms in these sentences.

1 The salary increase given to staff in previous years has little long-term impact on motivation.

2 Maslow's theory of motivation are differ from that of Vroom's.

3 Rational decision-making models are popular in the 1950s, but are largely considered inaccurate today.

4 Whilst Herzberg's theory is based on only a limited sample, there had been much empirical support for theory.

5 Fayol has based his theory largely on his own personal experience of working in a company in the late 1800s.

2 Correct the mistakes with subject–verb agreement in these sentences.

1 Leadership are referred to as motivating and influencing people's performance so that it is at a higher level.

2 The concept take the majority of its ideas from previous concepts in the field.

3 Praise play a major role in the motivational methods used by many managers.

4 Non-monetary rewards has been shown to have a longer-lasting motivational impact than monetary ones.

5 Management are a field of study in many business schools.

3 Add the missing preposition to each of these sentences.

1 All managers should provide staff the appropriate amount of challenge for their role.

2 According to Maslow, people do not think creativity until they have fulfilled earlier needs, such as being part of a team.

3 Companies, governments and individuals are all focused in studies of ethical behaviour.

4 The increased workloads of many people today have led increasing levels of stress.

5 Negative changes in the economy can have an effect people's effort and motivation at work.

4 Correct the mistakes with word formation in these sentences.

1 In conclude, whilst the theory has played an important role in the development of the field, it has largely been discredited.

2 It is logically that companies wish to make the greatest use of non-monetary rewards.

3 Finance rewards have limited long-term impact on motivation.

4 Many people visual aspects of a project before implementing changes.

5 The administration load of some teachers can impact negatively on their job satisfaction.

5 Correct the mistakes with articles in these sentences.

1 The language ability, particularly in English, is essential in many careers.

2 Pfeffer regards workforce as a source of strategic advantage, not as a cost to be minimized.

3 A term *empowerment* refers to the idea of giving people greater control and responsibility.

4 Job enrichment model formulated by Hackman and Oldham (1980) suggested that managers could change a job's design to increase employee satisfaction.

5 The equity theory is commonly associated with J. Stacey Adams.

6 Compare your answers to Exercises 1–5 with a partner.

Unit extension

1 Look at this essay question again. Brainstorm and organize your own ideas on it.

> Allowing people to be creative and to make their own decisions are the most effective tools for motivating employees. Discuss.

2 Two theories of motivation were mentioned briefly in this unit – Maslow and Herzberg. Do some research on them. How do they relate to the essay question above?

3 How could you fit the two theories into your essay plan? Has your reading highlighted a need to change your ideas?

3 Language learning

- Writing thesis statements and maintaining line of argument
- Distinguishing fact from opinion
- Using past and present tenses
- Describing visually presented information
- Word formation
- Checking spelling and punctuation

Topic focus

1 Look at the languages above and answer these questions.

1 How many of these languages can you recognize?

2 How many languages can you speak?

3 Why did you decide to learn these languages?

4 Which languages do you think are the most important in the world today?

5 Have these languages always been important?

2 Which language do you think these statements are about?

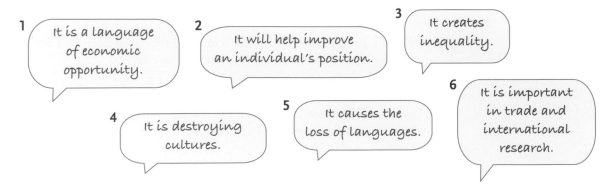

1 It is a language of economic opportunity.

2 It will help improve an individual's position.

3 It creates inequality.

4 It is destroying cultures.

5 It causes the loss of languages.

6 It is important in trade and international research.

3 Divide the statements in Exercise 2 into positive and negative opinions about the English language, then discuss these questions.

1 Which opinions do you agree with?

2 Who might voice these opinions?

Essay structure and organization: thesis statements and line of argument

Study tip
A thesis statement is important in an essay which requires an opinion. Good thesis statements demonstrate the author's opinion clearly and usually come towards the end of the introduction.

1 Look at this essay question and the opinions on it below (a–d). Then answer the questions that follow.

> English is responsible for the death of languages and cultures around the world. To what extent do you agree with this statement?

a The growth of English has affected languages and cultures of the world.

b English has caused the death of languages and cultures around the world; however, this impact is limited largely to those countries in which English is a first language.

c English has not caused the death of languages and cultures around the world; rather, it has merged with these to create new and unique cultures.

1 Which opinion agrees with the statement in the essay question?

2 Which opinion disagrees with it?

3 Which opinion neither agrees nor disagrees?

2 Look at the plan below and decide whether all parts are clearly linked to the essay question in Exercise 1 and this thesis statement.

Globalization has caused the death of cultures and languages; English just happened to be the dominant language at the time of these two events.

Study tip
Thesis statements can also indicate the sub-topics which will be covered and the order in which they will appear.

> Paragraph 1: Definition of language/culture
> Paragraph 2: History of empires and their languages
> Paragraph 3: Impact of globalization on world cultures/languages
> Conclusion: Globalization, not English, caused death of other languages/cultures.

3 What are the sub-topics of these essay questions?

1 Artificial languages are unlikely to become a dominant world language, as there is no economic or political power behind them.

2 Although China has a strong economy and a vast number of native speakers, the lack of second-language learners and the status of the language in other countries means it is unlikely to become a global language.

3 English is likely to continue to be the world's main language; however, strong regional languages such as Arabic and Spanish are also likely to rise.

Connecting the thesis statement and the main body

4 Below are three suggestions for the main ideas for paragraphs in this essay question.

> Artificial languages are unlikely to become a dominant world language, as there is no economic or political power behind them.

1 Artificial languages became popular during the late 1800s through to the mid-1900s, the most famous of which is perhaps Esperanto.

2 Artificial languages were created largely through the fear of one language or culture coming to dominate and take over other cultures.

3 However, a language becomes dominant because of the economic and political importance of its speakers; therefore, a language without these features will struggle to gain a dominant status.

Choose one of the other two essay questions from Exercise 3 and write possible main ideas for each paragraph.

Critical thinking: distinguishing fact from opinion

1 Work in small groups. Discuss your opinions on these topics.

1 Girls are more successful language learners than boys.

2 Banning smoking in public places is the right thing to do.

3 Testing cosmetics on animals should be banned.

4 Hunting unless for food should be banned.

2 Were your opinions in Exercise 1 based on any facts? What facts could you use to support these opinions?

1 Humans are overfishing the seas.

2 People are dying younger because of weight issues.

3 Age is key in successful language learning.

4 A vegetarian diet is the healthiest diet.

 In academic writing, you are encouraged to provide your own opinion, but you always need to support it. This is commonly done by providing facts, statistics, quotes or examples.

3 Look at these paragraphs. Circle the opinions and underline the supporting facts.

The English language has more direct responsibility for language loss in its native-speaking countries. Canada, the USA and Australia each have a large number of indigenous languages within their borders which have already been lost or are on the verge of disappearance. In Australia, for example, more than 200 languages are thought to have been lost in recent years.

English is seen in many countries, at an individual, institutional or national level, as representing the key to economic opportunity. In China, for example, the role and status of English 'is higher than ever in history, as evidenced by its position as a key subject in the curriculum, and as a crucial determinant for university entrance and procuring well-paid jobs in the commercial sector' (Adamson, 2002, p.241; see also Hu, 2002).

4 Read these facts. For each one, write an opinion you think it could be supporting.

1 It has over 400 million native speakers and nearly one billion people speak it as a second language.

2 Nearly 25% of the UK population are considered to be obese.

3 It is estimated that the world's supplies of oil will only last for another 40 years.

Language focus 1: using past and present tenses

1 Read the text and underline the verbs. Which verb tenses are used the most?

Calculations of linguistic diversity and the current viability of languages are fraught with problems. Some linguists might argue with the figure of 6,000–7,000 plus or minus a few hundred, but few would take issue with it in round terms. The majority of these languages, however, are located in a few countries, and they tend to be spoken by small groups of people who have little political or cultural power within the sovereign states in which they live. For example, in 1983, a report to UNESCO calculated that 20–25 per cent of the world's languages are to be found in Oceania, but that they were spoken by between only 0.1 and 0.2 per cent of the world's population (Dixon, 1991). Overall, over 80 per cent of the world's languages are spoken by fewer than 5 per cent of its population.

2 Match the main uses of the present and past simple (1–5) to the correct example sentences (a–e).

1 present state

2 repeated action/habit

3 general truth

4 past state

5 past habit/action

a Now, Mandarin is regarded by many Chinese speakers in Hong Kong as the more important second language to learn.

b Tests for English are taken every year in many countries of the world.

c Many artificial languages were created.

d Papua New Guinea has over 800 languages.

e French was considered a global language in the 18th century.

3 Complete each of these sentences with the correct form of the verb in brackets. Some sentences require a passive structure.

1 In the 18th century, French _____ (consider) a global language.

2 English _____ (be) a global language.

3 Esperanto _____ (create) to become a global language.

4 There _____ (be) more than one billion speakers of English worldwide.

5 French, German and English _____ (have) the special status of being the working languages of Europe.

6 Twenty-two countries _____ (account) for some 5,000 of the world's 6,000 languages.

4 Write three sentences about the current status of languages around the world. If you need any ideas, look at Exercise 1 again or the *Using sources* section on page 30.

5 Write three sentences about the status of languages in the past.

Using sources: describing visually presented information

1 Write these terms in the correct column of the table below.

axis   bar chart   chart   column   double   dramatic   gradual   graph
key   legend   peak   plummet   rapid   row   slight   steady   table

type of visual	part of a visual	type of change

2 Look at the pie charts below and complete these sentences using words from Exercise 1.

1 The information is presented in two _____ .

2 The percentage of Chinese-speaking Internet users in 2005 was more than _____ the number in 2000.

3 The percentage of German-speaking Internet users has remained _____ .

4 The number of other language users showed a _____ rise between 2000 and 2005.

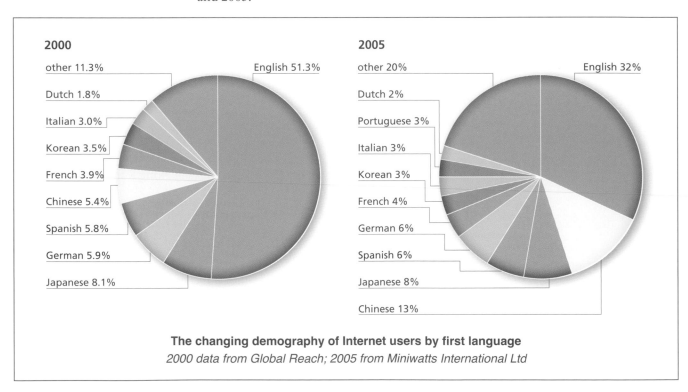

2000

other 11.3%
Dutch 1.8%
Italian 3.0%
Korean 3.5%
French 3.9%
Chinese 5.4%
Spanish 5.8%
German 5.9%
Japanese 8.1%
English 51.3%

2005

other 20%
Dutch 2%
Portuguese 3%
Italian 3%
Korean 3%
French 4%
German 6%
Spanish 6%
Japanese 8%
Chinese 13%
English 32%

The changing demography of Internet users by first language
2000 data from Global Reach; 2005 from Miniwatts International Ltd

3 Use phrases from the box to complete the description below of the two pie charts.

according to	from ... to	increased	plummeted	show

The charts **1** _____ the changing demography of Internet users by first language. **2** _____ the first pie chart, nearly 50% of Internet users in 2000 spoke English as a first language. However, by 2005, this number had **3** _____ to only one-third of users speaking English as a first language. Chinese-speaking users **4** _____ the most significantly, **5** _____ 5.4% _____ 13% of users. In addition, the percentage of users speaking 'other' languages rose from one in ten to one in five.

4 Choose other information from the two pie charts and extend the description in Exercise 3.

Language focus 2: word formation

1 **Match these words (1–4) to their definitions (a–d).**

1	creation	**a**	the efficient use of money
2	economically	**b**	a possible or probable amount
3	estimated	**c**	something that someone has made
4	evaluate	**d**	to judge or determine the value or amount of something

2 a **Add the words from Exercise 1 to this table.**

verb	noun	adjective	adverb
			creatively
economize			
estimate			
	evaluation evaluator		

b **Complete the rest of the table.**

3 **Using the examples in the table in Exercise 2, identify common endings for each word form (verb, noun, adjective and adverb). What other endings do you know?**

4 **Use the correct form of the words in brackets to complete these sentences.**

1 Whilst the ideas were strong in terms of logic, they lacked .... (*create*).

2 The decisions were made for .... (*economize*) reasons rather than political ones.

3 The .... (*estimate*) costs were not in line with the actual costs.

4 It is difficult to .... (*evaluate*) the number of speakers of English as a second or foreign language accurately.

5 The .... (*economize*) grew faster than expected.

6 It is .... (*estimate*) that nearly 200 languages die every year.

7 The .... (*evaluate*) was not as accurate as hoped.

8 The Internet could be considered one of the greatest .... (*create*) of the last 100 years, considering the impact it has had on modern daily life.

5 **Select another word from this unit that was new to you. Create your own sentences to demonstrate the different forms of this word.**

Evaluating writing: spelling and punctuation

Punctuation **1 Match the punctuation symbols (1–6) to their names (a–f).**

1 .   **a** exclamation mark

2 ,   **b** full stop

3 ?   **c** colon

4 !   **d** question mark

5 ;   **e** comma

6 :   **f** semi-colon

2 Work with a partner to answer these questions.

1 Which of the symbols in Exercise 1 is rarely used in academic writing?

2 Which is only occasionally used in academic writing?

3 For which ones do you know some or all of the rules of usage? What are they?

3 Add commas to these sentences in the correct places.

1 English is a global language but this status may not continue.

2 Whilst studying English she lived in the USA.

3 However she made little progress.

4 Esperanto which is one of many invented languages is spoken by few people.

4 Correct the use of capital letters in these sentences. One sentence is correct.

1 One billion people speak english as a second language.

2 it has been argued that english has caused the disappearance of a number of languages.

3 According to smith (2004), some 2,000 languages are endangered.

4 Most endangered languages are in the pacific ocean region.

5 Many new languages were created during the Industrial Revolution.

6 unesco would like to preserve endangered languages.

Spelling **5 Correct the spelling in each of these commonly misspelled words.**

1 acheive	6 finaly
2 apparantly	7 incidently
3 arguement	8 occured
4 definately	9 accomodate
5 enviroment	10 basicly

6 Which word is spelt incorrectly in each of these groups of words?

1 appearence   believe   business

2 calendar   compltly   conscious

3 existence   familiar   foriegn

4 hierarchy   guarantee   foward

5 gaurd   immediately   independent

6 knowledge   neccessary   occurrence

7 Correct the punctuation and spelling mistakes in this text.

english has acheived a status as the world's global language. A number of arguements have been put foward as to why a language spoken by only a small group of native speakers has achieved such a status. One of the main arguments is the economic dominence and importance of the USA. However the roots are arguably much earlier than this and are linked to factors such as the industrial revolution. Whilst english is still considered the world's global language today it's widely debated as to weather this will continue.

Unit extension

1 Research a language that is in danger of dying.

2 Is anything being done to protect this language?

3 Use this language as an example to write a short essay on the topic.

Languages in danger of dying are being protected and should continue to be protected. Discuss.

4 Sustainability

Aims

- Writing an effective introduction
- Producing logical arguments – reasons and conclusions
- Word formation
- Paraphrasing text
- Self-editing

Topic focus

1 Discuss these questions with a partner.

1 What's your favourite food?

2 Which country's food do you like best?

3 What things might people consider when they buy food?
Example: cost

4 What factors do you personally consider?

2 Look at the images below and discuss these questions with a partner.

1 What is the first thought that comes into your mind when you see each image?

2 What do you think connects each of these topics?

3 Have you heard of the concept 'food miles'?

3 a Look at this essay question and underline the key words.

> Local and seasonal food should be subsidized by the government in order to encourage people to live a more sustainable lifestyle. Discuss.

b Brainstorm your ideas for answering the question with a partner.

c Organize your ideas into a logical structure.

Essay structure and organization: writing an effective introduction

1 **Read this introduction and answer the questions below.**

> Sustainability is an important area to study, as it impacts on many things. It is also debatable as to whose responsibility sustainability is. However, sustainability is an exciting and interesting field to study.

1 What is the topic of the essay?

2 What might the question or title of the essay be?

3 What do you think the main points in the essay will be?

4 What is the reason for writing?

2 a **Work with a partner and brainstorm ideas for this essay question. Think about the questions below.**

> The world has reached its capacity in terms of the number of people it can support. Unless people dramatically change their behaviour, we are in danger of destroying the world. To what extent do you agree?

- Has the world reached its capacity?
- What behaviours do people need to change?
- What else (other than people's behaviour) could change?

b **Check with another pair that your ideas are clear. You will use this information later in the unit to help you write an effective introduction.**

> **ⓘ** Introductions follow many patterns, depending on essay length, subject area and the type of essay question. However, these features are common to many introductions:
> - getting the reader's interest, e.g. a quotation, a question, an interesting fact, a definition or general background information
> - more specific information related to the essay's topic
> - a thesis statement, stating the writer's point of view
> - an indication of the essay's structure.
> Typically, an introduction should be 'general leading to specific'.

3 a **Look again at the essay question from page 34 and re-order the sentences below and on page 36 (a–e) so that they form a logical introduction.**

> Local and seasonal food should be subsidized by the government in order to encourage people to live a more sustainable lifestyle. Discuss.

a Firstly, this essay will look at the advantages and disadvantages of consuming local and seasonal food, and whether governments should subsidize it. Secondly, this essay will look at other changes required to make lifestyles more sustainable.

b Food consumed in Western Europe can travel thousands of miles to reach dinner tables. The average British Sunday roast travels nearly 13,000 miles to reach British dinner plates.

c Countries such as Britain only produce enough food to be self-sufficient for four months of the year, so clearly consumption habits need to change.

     d This essay will argue that consuming seasonal and local food is only one step towards sustainability. Other factors, such as manufacturing methods, farming methods and transportation, also need to change.

     e However, changing food consumption habits alone is not enough to create a sustainable world.

  b Compare your answer with a partner.

4 a Look at the introduction below for this essay question and make a list of its weaknesses.

> Individual choices have the most impact on sustainability. Discuss.

> *What makes one choice more sustainable than another? For a long time, environmentalists have discussed the role of personal choice and its impact on sustainability. This essay will look at the role of personal choice in sustainability.*

  b Compare your answer with a partner.

5 a Look at these thesis statements and decide if they are weak or strong.

     1 Some people believe that the world's population is too big, whereas others do not.

     2 To be a successful language learner, motivation is more important than age.

     3 In order to assess the impact of bio fuel, we need to consider more factors than simply pollution.

     4 Internet shopping is very popular in my country.

     5 Encouraging people to be aware of their energy use is one of the best ways to solve the world's pollution and future energy shortages.

     6 There are several disadvantages to studying in the UK, but there are also many advantages.

  b Compare your answer with a partner.

6 a Write a thesis statement for each of these two essay questions.

> Improving public transport is key to reducing pollution. Discuss.

> Each individual's consumption should be limited by law. To what extent do you agree with this statement?

  b Evaluate your partner's thesis statement. Is it strong or weak?

7 a The introduction in Exercise 1 was a student's introduction to the essay question in Exercise 2. Rewrite it so that it is more suitable.

  b Compare your introduction with the typical features of introductions listed on page 35. Have you covered these?

8 Now write a full introduction for each of the essay questions in Exercise 6.

Critical thinking: producing logical arguments – reasons and conclusions

Study tip
Conclusions can be drawn at a number of points in an essay, not just at its end. Often each paragraph will have a concluding sentence.

1 **Conclusions have a number of functions. In terms of critical thinking, which of these do you think is the best definition of a conclusion?**

   a A summary of the main ideas discussed

   b A prediction of future events

   c A drawing-together of arguments, making a reasoned judgement

> *i* In some cases, a concluding sentence can be the first sentence of a paragraph, followed by the reasons. However, the most common structure is to:
> 1 state your position
> 2 provide your reasons
> 3 finish with a logical conclusion.
> It is important that your conclusion logically follows your reasons.

2 **Put these words and phrases in the correct column of the table below.**

first   similarly   in addition   alternatively   however   on the other hand
therefore   initially   by contrast   in the same way   this indicates   although
likewise   also   it might be argued that   as a result   it can be inferred
it can be deduced   even though   despite

introducing a line of reasoning	supporting a line of reasoning	presenting an alternative view	concluding

3 a **Read this paragraph and find any weaknesses in the reasoning or language used.**

> Firstly, food consumption levels in America are much higher than those in many other parts of the world. One reason could be the availability of fast and convenience foods. On the other hand, Americans also work a greater number of hours than many other countries. In addition, a lack of exercise results in poor diet choices. Therefore, American food consumption levels are likely to decrease if convenience foods were less available.

   b **Rewrite the paragraph so that the argument is more logical.**

4 a **Write a reasoned and logically concluded paragraph using this topic.**

   Secondly, an increasing reliance on cars is impacting on America's sustainability.

   b **The paragraph in Exercise 3 and the one you have just written are based on personal opinion. What support would you need to find to strengthen the arguments?**

Language focus: word formation

1 **Look at this article title. What do you think the article will be about?**

The future of food: A community response to a global problem

2 **These are some of the most common content words in the article. Do they relate to your ideas from Exercise 1?**

active   agriculture   **community**   concern   **consumer**   **economic**   grow
involve   local   more   people   produce   support   **sustain**   work

3 **The words in bold in Exercise 2 are from the Academic Word List. Complete this table with the different forms of each word.**

verb	noun	adjective	adverb
	1 consumer 2	1 2	
	community		
	1 2	economic	
involve			
sustain			

4 **Complete these sentences using words from the table in Exercise 3.**

1 ＿＿＿＿＿＿ levels in Western Europe are much higher than much of Africa.

2 The European Union is one economic and political ＿＿＿＿＿＿ .

3 To ＿＿＿＿＿＿ effort over such a long period of time requires dedication.

4 Public ＿＿＿＿＿＿ is key to the success of the policy.

5 An ＿＿＿＿＿＿ car can save money and help protect the environment.

5 **Write a sentence of your own using each of the words from Exercise 3.**

Prefixes 6 **Discuss the meaning of these prefixes with a partner. What words do you know that begin with each of these prefixes?**

1 bio–   2 eco–   3 ir–   4 mis–   5 non–   6 over–   7 re–   8 un–

7 **Complete each of these sentences using one of the prefixes from Exercise 6.**

1 Many ＿＿＿-systems in the world are in danger due to human activity.

2 Many people's level of consumption is ＿＿＿sustainable.

3 Agricultural ＿＿＿management has caused poor food production levels in some areas.

4 Many countries are ＿＿＿populated and cannot sustain their population.

5 ＿＿＿cycling is key to reducing consumption.

6 Reducing ＿＿＿-diversity means we will eventually become weaker as a planet.

7 Our reliance on ＿＿＿-renewable resources needs to change.

8 Many of the effects of pollution are ＿＿＿reversible.

8 **Write a new sentence using each of the prefixes in Exercise 6.**

Using sources: paraphrasing text

1 **Decide which of these statements about paraphrasing are true (T) and which are false (F).**

1 Paraphrasing uses the exact words of the text.

2 Paraphrasing shows how your own ideas have been developed by your reading.

3 Paraphrasing is used because too many direct quotes are not appropriate.

4 Paraphrasing expresses complex ideas in a clear and simple way.

5 Paraphrasing should clearly support the point you are making.

6 Paraphrasing from a book is easier than paraphrasing from your notes.

7 Paraphrasing should copy the style of the original text.

2 **Read this statement and decide whether the paraphrase below is suitable. Why? / Why not?**

Technological improvements such as greater fuel efficiency merely lead to greater consumption of a product – people drive more, for example.

Technological advancements such as greater fuel efficiency only lead to increased consumption of a product – people fly more, for example.

3 a **This paragraph is difficult to understand and is a good example of text that could be paraphrased. Spend some time with a dictionary and a partner to try to work out its meaning.**

The eco-efficiency of the economy is improving through 'dematerialization', the increased productivity of resource inputs, and the reduction of wastes discharged per unit of output. However, eco-efficiency is not improving fast enough to prevent impacts from rising.

b **Read this paraphrase of the above paragraph. Match sections of the paraphrase to the original text.**

The environmental efficiency of the economy is improving in two ways. Firstly, less energy is being used in production; and secondly, less waste is being produced. However, the change is too slow, and the impact is still increasing.

> **Study tip**
> When paraphrasing, try to make notes first and then paraphrase from your notes. You are less likely to plagiarize and will also produce a style that fits well into your normal style of writing.

4 a **Read this text and take notes from it.**

Levels of GDP (Gross Domestic Product) were once used as the sole means to compare standards of living in different countries. Essentially, this comparison implied that if you had more money, you could consume more and thus have a higher standard of living. Today, the more commonly accepted measure is the HDI (Human Development Index). Whilst this does still take GDP into account, it also considers two other factors. These are the average life expectancy at birth and the average number of years' education each person recieves. Thus quality of life is not only based on the ability to consume products but also to live a long, healthy and educated life, and consumption of products does not necessarily lead to an increased standard of living.

b **Look at your partner's notes. Use the effective note-taking tips in Unit 1 to evaluate your partner's notes.**

5 a **Look at this opinion and use your notes from Exercise 4 to create a paraphrase that supports it.**

Consumption of products does not necessarily lead to an increased standard of living.

b **Look at your partner's paraphrase and answer these questions.**

1 Does the paraphrase sound like their own style of writing?

2 Is the paraphrase different enough from the original?

3 If it is too similar to the original, how could they change it, e.g. vocabulary, word formation, word order?

4 Does it clearly support the statement?

6 **Read this paragraph. What is the function of each sentence?**

Achieving a work–life balance not only helps to lower consumption levels, it can also impact on life satisfaction. According to a recent study, countries such as Denmark, the Netherlands, Finland and Sweden all pay attention to work–life balance and are also the four happiest countries in the world (De Graaf, 2010). Thus the benefits in reducing hours of work are not only environmental but also personal satisfaction.

7 **Create a similarly structured paragraph using your paraphrase from Exercise 5.**

Evaluating writing: self-editing

1 a **Read this checklist for question analysis.**

● Have I identified all the sections to the question?

● Have I identified the specific focus of the question?

● What is the meaning of the instruction word?

● What style of writing is the essay looking for, e.g. evaluative/descriptive?

● Is it clear what is expected of me in this essay?

b **Below is a student's evaluation of this essay question. Do you agree with their evaluation according to the above checklist?**

The world has reached its capacity in terms of the number of people it can support. Unless people dramatically change their behaviour, we are in danger of destroying the world. To what extent do you agree?

The essay is asking for an evaluation of the opinion stated in the question. The main body will look at two main halves – has the world reached its capacity? If it has, do people need to change their behaviour, or is there another way?

2 **Use this checklist for evaluating an introduction to review the introductions you wrote in Exercise 8 on page 36.**

● Does the introduction go from general to specific?

● It is engaging to the reader? (Underline the part you think is particularly engaging.)

● Is there a thesis statement? (Underline it.)

● Is the opinion in the thesis statement clear? (Try to express this in another way.)

3 a Look back at the work you did on these topics. For each one, write a list of four things you think you should check.

   1 paraphrasing   2 summary writing   3 logical arguments

   b Compare your checklist with a partner. Could you use your partner's checklist? Why? / Why not?

4 List these topics in the order you would check them. Then discuss with a partner why you would check in this order.

   a content is relevant to the question

   b grammar, spelling and vocabulary

   c essay structure

   d paragraph logic

   e use of sources and bibliography

Unit extension

1 Find a text related to this essay question.

> Changing to renewable energy is not enough; people also need to change their energy consumption. To what extent do you agree?

2 Select two parts of the text you have found that you think you could include in the essay and write suitable paraphrases of them.

3 Develop your paraphrases into full paragraphs.

4 Write a suitable introduction to the essay question.

5 Bring the text you found, your two paragraphs and your introduction to the next class. Work with a partner and answer these questions.

   1 Is the paraphrase introduced?

   2 Does the paraphrase support the opening sentence?

   3 Has your partner commented on the significance of the paraphrase?

   4 Does the introduction go from general to specific?

   5 Is there a clear thesis statement?

5 Crime

Aims

- Writing topic sentences
- Using modals and hedging language
- Evaluating supporting evidence and examples
- Giving supporting examples
- Alternative and counter-arguments
- Hedging and academic language

Topic focus

1 Discuss this question with a partner.

Do you think the level of crime in your country has decreased, increased or stayed the same in the last 20 years? Do you think there is a reason for this?

2 Look at this graph. Why do you think the crimes people talk about are much higher than those actually reported to the police? Brainstorm your ideas with a partner.

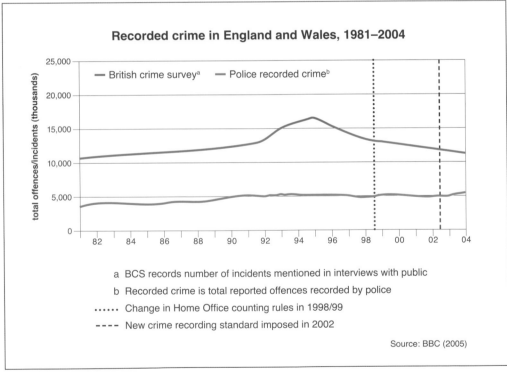

Recorded crime in England and Wales, 1981–2004

- a BCS records number of incidents mentioned in interviews with public
- b Recorded crime is total reported offences recorded by police
- ...... Change in Home Office counting rules in 1998/99
- ---- New crime recording standard imposed in 2002

Source: BBC (2005)

3 a Would you report all crimes to the police? Think about the following:

- Someone you know is driving too fast.
- Your mobile phone is stolen.
- Your house is burgled.

b Explain your reasons to a partner.

1 **Look at these two paragraphs. The topic sentence in Paragraph A has been underlined. Underline the topic sentence in paragraph B.**

A

As measured by statistics of crimes reported to the police, rates of crime in the UK increased enormously over the 20th century. Prior to the 1920s, there were fewer than 100,000 offences recorded each year in England and Wales; this number had reached 500,000 by 1950, and peaked at 5.6 million by 1992. Levels of recorded crime more than doubled between 1977 and 1992.

B

Since the mid-1990s, the number of crimes committed in the UK overall appears to have levelled off. Measures such as the British Crime Survey have shown a considerable fall in the amount of crime. According to recent data, the risk of becoming a victim of crime is at its lowest for more than 20 years (Clegg et al., 2005). The end to rising crime figures has taken many experts by surprise. The cause behind it, and whether this trend is sustainable, is still uncertain.

2 a **Choose the correct topic sentence (a–b) to complete each paragraph (1–2) below.**

a Despite recent falls shown in the statistics on crime, there remains a widespread perception amongst the population that, over time, crime has grown more prevalent and serious (Nicholas et al., 2005).

b To determine the extent of crime and the most common forms of criminal offence, one approach is to examine the official statistics on the number of crimes which the police actually record.

1

Recently, it has been reported that levels of worry about the main types of crime have been falling, although anxiety about anti-social behavior remains more stable (Clegg et al., 2005). If at one time crime was seen as something marginal or exceptional, in recent decades it has become a more prominent concern in many people's lives. Surveys show that people are now much more fearful of crime than in earlier times and are experiencing heightened anxiety about going out after dark, about their homes being burgled and about becoming victims of violence. People are reportedly also more worried about low-level kinds of disorder, such as graffiti, drunken rowdiness and groups of teenagers hanging out on the streets.

2

Since such statistics are published regularly, there would seem to be no difficulty in assessing crime rates – but this assumption is quite wrong. Statistics about crime and delinquency are probably the least reliable of all officially published figures on social issues. Criminologists have emphasized that we cannot take statistics on crime at face value.

b Look at the final sentence in paragraph 2.

Does this:

a summarize the main idea of the paragraph?

b draw a logical conclusion of the paragraph?

c lead into the next idea/paragraph?

3 These two paragraphs lead on from paragraph 2 on page 43. Write a suitable topic sentence for each of them.

There are many reasons that people decide not to report a crime. Even in cases where a victim is wounded, more than half the cases are not reported to the police; victims claim, for example, that it is a private affair or something they have dealt with themselves. Crime may go unreported for other reasons. Some people assume that the crime is too trivial to be taken to the police, or think that the police wouldn't be able to do anything about it anyway. A large proportion of car theft is reported, however, because the owner needs to have done so in order to claim on insurance policies.

It has been estimated that although 43% of crimes do get reported to police, just 29% are recorded; this figure does, however, vary depending on the crime (BCS 2002/3). This can occur for a number of reasons. The police may be sceptical of the validity of some information about purported crimes that comes their way, or the victim may not want to lodge a formal complaint.

Language focus 1: using modals and hedging language

1 Find words or phrases from the box that appear in the paragraph below.

it is unlikely that	can	tend to	could	it appears to	
may	it seems that	there is a tendency to	possibility	
relatively	conceivably	generally	perhaps	might	

It is unlikely that crime statistics show the true pattern of crime for a number of reasons. Firstly, relatively few crimes that are committed are actually reported. This may be for a number of reasons, such as people feeling that the police might not take their crime seriously or that perhaps they feel that they have dealt with it themselves. It could also be due to factors such as the individual not feeling that the crime is serious enough to report. Secondly, there is a tendency to use these statistics in either the media or for political purposes to influence the public's views. Governments tend to want to show that crime rates are falling in order to show that their policies are working. However, generally speaking, there are a number of reasons why crime rates change, and these changes are perhaps due to reasons other than government policy.

2 a Put the words/phrases from the box in Exercise 1 into the correct column of this table.

adverbs	nouns / noun phrases	verbs / verb phrases

b Which of the verbs are modal verbs?

c Can you add any other words or phrases to each category?

d Put the words/phrases in order of probability, from the most to the least probable.

3 a Put these phrases in the correct column of the table below.

most   a number of   normally   usually   a few   few   several   frequently
hardly ever   a minority   a majority   some   regularly   occasionally

quantity	frequency

b Can you think of any other phrases for these categories?

c Put the words/phrases in order, from the biggest to the smallest, and the most frequent to the least frequent.

4 Rewrite these sentences using the phrases in brackets to make the sentences more cautious.

1 Crimes are not reported. (*a number of* / *might*)

2 All minor crimes are ignored. (*several* / *might be*)

3 The police do not believe the information they receive from people. (*might not* / *a few*)

4 Government statistics show every year that crime rates are falling. (*tend to* / *constantly*)

5 Crime   45

Critical thinking: supporting evidence and examples

1 a A student has used information from the graph on page 42 in this essay extract. There are a number of weaknesses in the way the information has been used. Read the extract and discuss the questions below.

> Crime in the UK is becoming less significant, as crime rates are falling year on year. The British Crime Survey (BBC, 2005) shows that crime fell every year from 1995 to 2004 and has fallen from 16 million incidents to 11 million incidents per year. This near-30% fall in the number of crimes committed shows that whilst crime is still a concern, it is much less of a concern than in previous years.

1 Just because there are fewer crimes, does this mean they are less significant?

2 Has the type of crime changed?

3 What research method was used to collect this data? Who did they ask? Where? When?

4 Was it correct to select this information and ignore the recorded crime?

5 Does this line on the graph actually show the rate of crime?

b Look at the extract below, in which another student has used the same graph in a different way. Work with a partner to develop questions that highlight the weaknesses in the way this student has used the information.

Example: What do they mean by serious? Do total numbers equal seriousness?

> Crime in the UK is no more serious today than it was a decade ago. Between 1992 and 2004, the official rate of recorded crime showed little change (BBC, 2005). Thus, whilst there is the perception that society has become more dangerous, the statistics do not support this claim.

2 a Look at the paragraphs on pages 43–44 on topic sentences. What examples can you find to support each of these opinions?

1 Crime rates in the UK increased dramatically in the past.

2 People are more worried about crime in the UK than in the past.

3 Crimes are not always reported.

b What might be the weakness of the evidence or examples you have selected?

Using sources: giving supporting examples

1 a **Underline the language in these sentences used to give an example.**

1 Car crime, for example, is usually reported, as people need to do so to make a claim on their insurance.

2 Not all crime is reported; this is exemplified by the difference between the figures in the British Crime Survey and those actually recorded by the police.

3 Minor crimes, such as pick-pocketing or speeding, are rarely reported.

4 Today, more people are worried about crime than in the past; this is illustrated by the results in a number of surveys in which people are more worried about violent crime and more scared to go out alone after dark.

5 A potential fall in the rate of crime is shown by the British Crime Survey.

6 In the case of Britain, recorded levels of crime have significantly increased.

b **Can you think of any other language of exemplification? Use these prompts to help you.**

1 s _ _ _ s t _ _ s
2 e x _ _ _ l i _ _ _ _ t _ i _
3 i l l _ _ _ _ _ t e s t h _ _
4 f _ _ i n _ _ _ _ c e
5 b y w _ _ o f i l l _ _ _ _ _ _ i o n

c **In which of the sentences in Exercise 1a are the examples the main information, and in which are they additional information?**

d **Circle the commas. Can you write two rules for comma use in these structures?**

2 **Complete the gaps in these sentences with expressions from Exercise 1. More than one phrase might be possible.**

1 Not all crime is considered equally seriously, and the range of crime reported _____ to be the case.

2 Changes in the perception of the risk of crime is _____ the fact that more people are afraid of violent crime today than they were in the past.

3 Crime statistics have a number of uses; _____ , governments may want to show that there has been a reduction in the levels of crime committed.

4 The government wanted to show serious crime had reduced and, _____ , highlighted the reduction in violent crimes committed.

3 **Give examples of the following using language from this section.**

1 Crime rates in the UK increased dramatically in the past.

2 People are more worried about crime in the UK than in the past.

3 Crimes are not always reported.

Language focus 2: alternative and counter-arguments

1 Put these expressions in the correct column of the table below.

at the same time   even though   furthermore   however   in addition
moreover   nonetheless   not only … but also   on the other hand

adding support	adding a counter-argument

2 Choose the correct alternative to complete each of these sentences.

1 English is considered to be the world's global language; *however / in addition*, it is debatable that it will maintain such a status as other languages become important.

2 The role of a leader can be quite different, depending on the culture the person is working in. *Moreover / On the other hand*, the distance between a leader and their staff can vary greatly.

3 *Neither / Not only* wind power *nor / but also* solar power has been shown to be a reliable source of energy in all parts of the world.

4 Increased consumption and *at the same time / nonetheless* increased dependency on private transport have had a serious impact on the environment.

5 *Even though / Furthermore* formative assessment is a valuable learning tool, many students fail to make full use of this.

3 a Read this essay question and brainstorm ideas for and against it with a partner. Use the texts from this unit to help you if necessary.

> The UK is becoming a more dangerous place. Discuss.

b Write a paragraph in support of the above statement and a paragraph against it. Try to use language from Exercise 1.

c Exchange paragraphs with your partner. Underline the connecting language. Do you think your partner has used the expressions correctly?

 It is often important for academic writing to consider a range of perspectives on an argument, and therefore conflicting arguments will often need to be presented. Your choice of cautious language helps show your position, so try not to use phrases that present the two arguments equally.

Evaluating writing: hedging and academic language

Study tip
Hedging can be important in academic writing, but it is also useful when giving feedback to peers so that your comments are polite.

1 Underline the language that makes each of these sentences more polite.

1 I think you might need to proofread for grammar mistakes.

2 You might need to change the focus of this paragraph.

3 The essay could perhaps be made stronger with more sources.

4 This quote perhaps doesn't fully support your opinion.

5 How about the ideas of Jackson, as they might be useful?

6 Do you mind if I make a suggestion for this section?

7 May I just make one more comment here?

2 a Complete this list of features from Unit 1 that can make language less formal.

1 p _ _ _ o n _ l
2 s u _ _ _ _ t i _ _
3 a s _ _ _ _ i v e
4 c o _ _ _ _ _ c t _ _ _ s
5 a c _ _ _ e v _ _ _ e
6 c o _ _ _ q u _ _ l v o _ _ _ _ l _ _ y

b Find examples of the above features in these texts.

A

I believe it's impossible to reduce the level of crime without strict methods of control. How can we possibly expect people to behave without severe threats? I know from my own personal experience that when a crime is punished harshly, the people don't do the same things again.

Without doubt, the biggest challenge for my government is controlling the levels of crime. The last government was, to be honest, a complete disaster. We all know the best methods to control crime, and unfortunately the government hasn't got a clue.

B

For sure, younger people learn languages better than older people. I learned French from a young age and I'm much better than my parents, who have only just started to learn it. Linguists have proven that kids are without doubt much better learners than adults. To even debate otherwise is just ridiculous.

3 a Work with a partner.

Student A: Imagine that you wrote Text A in Exercise 2.

Student B: Provide feedback on Text A, suggesting changes they could make. Try to use expressions from Exercise 1 to offer advice.

b Swap roles and do the same for Text B.

Unit extension

1 Research crime statistics in another country and make a note of your findings.

2 Look at the essay question below and, using your findings from Exercise 1, write one paragraph that describes changes in the level of crime, and another that describes changes in the type of crime. Include a topic sentence and examples in both paragraphs.

Describe the changes in the level and type of crime in one particular country. How have these changes affected society?

3 Bring your paragraphs to the next class and swap them with a partner. Underline the language your partner has used to introduce their example. How suitable are the examples? Does the example support the main idea well?

4 Use the polite phrases to provide feedback to your partner.

6 Revision

Essay structure and organization

Question analysis (Unit 1) 1 Write a definition of what each of these words is asking you to do in an essay.

   1 analyze   2 evaluate   3 outline   4 illustrate   5 justify   6 describe

2 What is the difference between these two essay questions and the expected answer?

a
> Describe two key theories of leadership.

b
> Evaluate two key theories of leadership.

Thesis statements and line of argument (Unit 3) 3 Which of the thesis statements below do you think is the best for this essay question, and why?

> Discuss the relevance of Fayol's theory to management today.

   a Whilst Fayol's theory of leadership presents some interesting ideas, its transferability is limited, because the theory is based solely on personal experience in a context, unlike many work environments of today.

   b Fayol's theory of leadership is interesting for managers in the world of business today.

   c Fayol's theory was developed after his experience of work in industrial France in the 20th century.

4 Use the mind map from Unit 2 (page 18) to help you write a thesis statement for this essay question.

> Allowing people to be creative and make their own decisions is the most effective tool for motivating employees. Discuss.

Writing an effective introduction (Unit 4)

5 Work with a partner. List four features of an effective introduction.

6 Put these sentences in the correct order to form an introduction.

a Many of these companies are hoping for synergy effects, so that they can cut costs of staffing, property and marketing.

b Often it is argued that these failures were to some extent expected or that they were caused by market conditions.

c Less than 50 per cent of companies achieve their objectives after being merged with another company.

d This essay will argue that this is not the case and that it is a failure of management to pay attention to differences in company culture and administrative procedures.

e However, few achieve their targets and often actually make financial losses rather than gains.

Topic sentences (Unit 5)

7 Write a topic sentence for each of these paragraphs.

1 Canada, the USA and Australia each have a large number of indigenous languages within their borders which have already been lost or are on the verge of disappearance. In Australia, for example, more than 200 languages are thought to have been lost in recent years. Furthermore, it is thought that this loss is likely to continue at a rapid rate in coming years.

2 In China, for example, the role and status of English 'is higher than ever in history, as evidenced by its position as a key subject in the curriculum, and as a crucial determinant for university entrance and procuring well-paid jobs in the commercial sector' (Adamson, 2002, p241; see also Hu, 2002). With more countries giving English an official status or adopting it as a key language of education, it is likely that this trend will continue.

Language focus

Register (Unit 1)

1 List six features of academic writing.

2 Underline the informal parts in each of these sentences.

1 Effective leaders perhaps shouldn't manage in such a traditional hierarchical manner in modern organizations.

2 I believe that empowering individuals is one of the most effective ways to improve creativity.

3 I interviewed 20 people for the survey.

4 It can be argued that kids learn languages better than adults.

5 I learned French from the age of five and achieved a higher level than my school friend who started at 11.

6 America is overpopulated.

3 Rewrite the sentences from Exercise 2 in a more academic style.

Present and past tense
(Unit 3)

4 Complete the paragraph below using the verbs in the box. Put the verbs into the correct form of present or past tense. Sometimes you will need a passive structure.

be	believe	develop	have	see	think	think

It **1** _____ during the industrial revolution, when manufacturing formed the basis of the economy, that a traditional hierarchical structure was the best method of management. Weber **2** _____ his bureaucratic management theory after observing such management methods in practice. It **3** _____ that clearly defined roles and a clear chain of command proved an effective management system. One criticism of the theory **4** _____ that it did not allow companies to adapt to customer needs and demands quickly. Today, more companies are customer focused, and this has had an impact on the methods of management used. Now it **5** _____ that employees thrive in an environment where they are empowered. Employees **6** _____ closer contact with their managers and key decision-makers. They **7** _____ as integral to a successful creative company as any other form of investment.

Word formation
(Units 3 and 4)

5 Complete each of these sentences with the correct form of the word in brackets.

1 The _____ (*lead*) of companies has changed dramatically in recent years.

2 Students who are _____ (*motivate*) to learn are more likely to be successful.

3 The same _____ (*statistic*) data can be used to support many different points of view.

4 A wide range of _____ (*assess*) take place in universities.

5 Decisions made for economic reasons might not always be _____ (*environment*) friendly.

6 Use another form of each of the words in Exercise 5 to create a sentence about each of the main themes of the units so far.

Alternative and counter-arguments (Unit 5)

7 Correct the mistakes with the use of linking language in these sentences.

1 He studied hard and was not successful in passing the course.

2 Despite assessment is not always seen as positive, most people accept it is needed.

3 English is spoken by some 1.8 billion people worldwide; furthermore, only 400 million of these are native speakers of English.

4 Levels of crime have not increased; moreover, people are more concerned about crime.

5 There are limited resources available for human consumption on this planet. On the other hand, the world has a capacity as to how many people it can support.

Critical thinking

Analyzing ideas (Unit 1) 1 a **Work with a partner. What different opinions might there be related to the opinion expressed in this essay question?**

> Crime statistics should not be reported unless a more effective method for collecting the data is found. Discuss.

b **Do you agree or disagree with the opinion?**

c **What questions would you need to ask to find evidence to prove or disprove this opinion?**

2 **Compare your questions from Exercise 1c with these questions. Do you agree that these are the right ones that need to be looked at? Why? / Why not?**

1 How are crime statistics reported?

2 Which crimes are most common?

3 Is the current method for collecting data ineffective?

4 What will be the benefits of not reporting crime statistics?

5 What types of crime are reported?

6 Who collects the data and reports the statistics? What bias might this create?

Evaluation of ideas 3 a **Work with a partner. Student A look at Paragraph A and Student B look at**
(Unit 2) **Paragraph B, then answer these questions.**

1 What is the possible limitation of this study?

2 What possible weaknesses are there in the study?

3 How could the study have been strengthened?

A

Maslow was a clinical psychologist who developed a theory of human motivation to help him understand the needs of his patients. He stressed the clinical sources of the theory and that it lacked experimental verification. Maslow did not claim that the hierarchy was a fixed or rigid scheme. His clinical experience suggested that most people have these needs in about this order.

B

Geert Hofstede is a Dutch academic who has conducted widely quoted studies of national cultural differences. The second edition of his research (Hofstede, 2001) extends and refines the conclusions of his original work, which was based on a survey of the attitudes of 116,000 IBM employees, one of the earliest global companies. The research inspired many empirical studies with non-IBM employees, in both the original countries in which IBM operated and in places where they did not. Kirkman et al. (2006) reviewed many of these and concluded that 'most of the country differences predicted by Hofstede were supported' (p.308).

b **Summarize your ideas for your partner.**

Fact and opinion (Unit 3) 4 **Read the text on page 54 and find information that supports each of these opinions.**

1 There is less crime in the UK today than there was 50 years ago.

2 Many people believe that there is more crime committed in the UK today.

3 Crime statistics are unreliable.

As measured by statistics of crimes reported to the police, rates of crime in the UK increased enormously over the 20th century. Prior to the 1920s, there were fewer than 100,000 offences recorded each year in England and Wales; this number had reached 500,000 by 1950, and peaked at 5.6 million by 1992. Levels of recorded crime more than doubled between 1977 and 1992.

Since the mid-1990s, the number of crimes committed in the UK overall appears to have leveled off. Measures such as the British Crime Survey have shown a considerable fall in the amount of crime (see Figure 1). According to recent data, the risk of becoming a victim of crime is at its lowest for more than 20 years (Clegg et al., 2005). The end to rising crime figures has taken many experts by surprise. The cause behind it, and whether this trend is sustainable, is still uncertain.

Despite recent falls shown in the statistics on crime, there remains a widespread perception amongst the population that, over time, crime has grown more prevalent and serious (Nicholas et al., 2005). Recently, it has been reported that levels of worry about the main types of crime have been falling, although anxiety about anti-social behaviour remains more stable (Clegg et al., 2005). If at one time crime was seen as something marginal or exceptional, in recent decades it has become a more prominent concern in many people's lives. Surveys show that people are now much more fearful of crime than in earlier times and are experiencing heightened anxiety about going out after dark, about their homes being burgled and about becoming victims of violence. People are reportedly also more worried about low-level kinds of disorder, such as graffiti, drunken rowdiness and groups of teenagers hanging out on the streets.

To determine the extent of crime and the most common forms of criminal offence, one approach is to examine the official statistics on the number of crimes which the police actually record. Since such statistics are published regularly, there would seem to be no difficulty in assessing crime rates – but this assumption is quite wrong. Statistics about crime and delinquency are probably the least reliable of all officially published figures on social issues. Criminologists have emphasized that we cannot take statistics on crime at face value.

Logical arguments (Unit 4)

5 a **Read this paragraph. Are there any weaknesses in the reasoning?**

Chinese is spoken by more people as a first language than any other language in the world. According to Ethnologue (2009), there are some 1.2 billion speakers of Chinese in the world. In addition, the Chinese economy is now the second largest in the world, with a value of $5.8 trillion (BBC, 2011). These two facts combined mean that Chinese is likely to become the world's number-one global language.

b **Rewrite the paragraph to make the argument more logical.**

Evidence and examples (Unit 5)

6 **Read this extract and how it has been used in the sentences below as supporting evidence. Which sentence has used the extract the most effectively? What are the weaknesses in the other two?**

Calculations of linguistic diversity and the current viability of languages are fraught with problems. Some linguists might argue with the figure of 6,000–7,000 plus or minus a few hundred, but few would take issue with it in round terms. The majority of these languages, however, are located in a few countries, and they tend to be spoken by small groups of people who have little political or cultural power within the sovereign states in which they live. For example, in 1983, a report to UNESCO calculated that 20–25 per cent of the world's languages are to be found in Oceania, but that they were spoken by between only 0.1 and 0.2 per cent of the world's population (Dixon, 1991). Overall, over 80 per cent of the world's languages are spoken by fewer than 5 per cent of its population.

David Graddol, *Endangered Languages* (2007)

a Linguistic diversity is rich throughout the world with, according to Graddol (2007), some 6,000–7,000 being widely used in the world today.

b A number of the world's languages may be in danger of becoming extinct due to the fact that they have so few speakers. Approximately 5% of the world speaks 80% of its languages (Graddol, 2007).

c Oceania has some 20–25% of the world's languages (Graddol, 2007); however, due to their geographic isolation, these languages are unlikely to survive.

Using sources

Summary writing (Unit 1) **1 Which of these sentences best summarizes the paragraph below?**

    a Today, crime is falling in the UK; however, people are more concerned about the threats of crime.

    b Statistics show that crime is falling in the UK.

Despite recent falls shown in the statistics on crime, there remains a widespread perception amongst the population that, over time, crime has grown more prevalent and serious (Nicholas et al., 2005). Recently, it has been reported that levels of worry about the main types of crime have been falling, although anxiety about anti-social behaviour remains more stable (Clegg et al., 2005). If at one time crime was seen as something marginal or exceptional, in recent decades it has become a more prominent concern in many people's lives. Surveys show that people are now much more fearful of crime than in earlier times and are experiencing heightened anxiety about going out after dark, about their homes being burgled and about becoming victims of violence. People are reportedly also more worried about low-level kinds of disorder, such as graffiti, drunken rowdiness and groups of teenagers hanging out on the streets.

2 a Take notes on this paragraph, then use your notes to write a brief summary.

To determine the extent of crime and the most common forms of criminal offence, one approach is to examine the official statistics on the number of crimes which the police actually record. Since such statistics are published regularly, there would seem to be no difficulty in assessing crime rates – but this assumption is quite wrong. Statistics about crime and delinquency are probably the least reliable of all officially published figures on social issues. Criminologists have emphasized that we cannot take statistics on crime at face value.

  b Compare your summary with that of a partner. Has your partner kept the meaning of the original?

Definitions (Unit 2) **3 Complete the sentences below using words from the box.**

building	communicating	data	enforces	increasing
highlighting	an organization	a person	a process	a tool

    1 Language is .... for .... our thoughts and feelings.

    2 A judge is .... who .... the law.

    3 Statistics are .... for .... social problems.

    4 Globalization is .... of .... trade around the world.

    5 UNESCO is .... for .... relationships between countries and cultures.

4 a **Look at this chart and write a brief description of the information in it.**

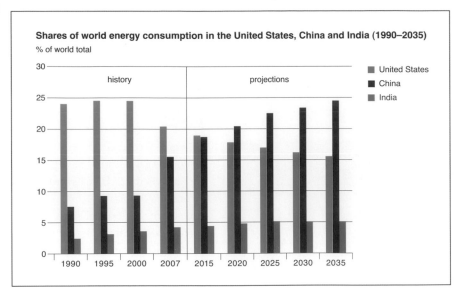

Shares of world energy consumption in the United States, China and India (1990–2035)
% of world total

b **Swap descriptions with a partner. Underline the words in your partner's description that describe change.**

5 **Look at this text and the paraphrase below. Match sections of the paraphrase to the original text.**

> McGregor presented two sets of assumptions underlying management practice: Theory X, which he called the traditional view of direction and control, and Theory Y, which suggests that people accept responsibility, and apply imagination, ingenuity and creativity to organizational problems. McGregor's work was based on Maslow's hierarchy of needs. He grouped Maslow's hierarchy into 'lower order' (Theory X) needs and 'higher order' (Theory Y) needs.

McGregor presented two hypotheses that lie beneath management practice – Theory X and Theory Y. The former follows the long-established view of a strong hierarchy, whereas the latter implies that people accept accountability, and show originality and inventiveness to company concerns. McGregor's work derives from Maslow's hierarchy of needs, with Theory X representing the bottom of Maslow's pyramid and Theory Y the top.

6 a **Take notes on this paragraph.**

> Since the mid-1990s, the number of crimes committed in the UK overall appears to have leveled off. Measures such as the British Crime Survey have shown a considerable fall in the amount of crime. According to recent data, the risk of becoming a victim of crime is at its lowest for more than 20 years (Clegg et al., 2005). The end to rising crime figures has taken many experts by surprise. The cause behind it, and whether this trend is sustainable, is still uncertain.

b **Use your notes to create a paraphrase that supports this statement.**

Crime rates in the UK have unexpectedly fallen.

c **Look at your partner's paraphrase and answer these questions.**

1 Does the paraphrase sound like their own style of writing?

2 Is the paraphrase different enough from the original?

3 If it is too similar to the original, how could they change it, e.g. vocabulary, word formation, word order?

4 Does it clearly support the statement?

Giving and supporting examples (Unit 5)

7 Complete the sentences below using the expressions in the box.

exemplified by	for instance	in the case of	such as

1 Languages _____ Chinese are an example of a common first language that is not frequently spoken by people as a second language.

2 A number of the world's languages are endangered by politically dominant languages. This is particularly _____ the threat English and Hindi pose to other languages in India.

3 _____ English, it was in the right place at the right time to become the world's number-one language.

4 In the past, second languages were often learned for political reasons, _____ Russian in much of Eastern Europe. Nowadays, many languages are learnt primarily for economic reasons.

Evaluating writing

Peer, teacher and student feedback

1 Discuss these questions with a partner.

1 What are the different things should you look at when evaluating your own work?

2 Which of these is more useful feedback? Why?
  a 'There are a lot of grammar mistakes.'
  b 'The introduction is very general and doesn't give a clear idea of your opinion.'

3 Which of these is the more polite way of providing feedback to a peer?
  a 'You need to include more support for your opinions.'
  b 'Have you considered including more support for your opinions?'

Grammar

2 a Correct the grammatical mistakes in these sentences.

1 Languages are learned more effective by motivated people.

2 A main language in Spain is Spanish.

3 The long-term needs of satisfy demands for energy supplies are not being met.

4 Before the merger, each individual have a lot of independence.

5 The company need to focus on growth and development to perform well.

b Compare your corrections with a partner.

Spelling

3 Correct the punctuation and spelling mistakes in this paragraph.

It is easy to put forward an arguement that china is increasingly responsible for much damage to the enviroment. Definately, china has had an increasing impact on the enviroment however it could also be argued that its industrial revolution will actually improve enviromental technology. Most technological advances in the world occured during industrial revolutions in other parts of the world such as in britain in the 1900s. Even, today china is using its technological progress to develop the neccesary technologies that will make part of Tianjin an enviromentally sustainable city.

7 Culture

- Structuring paragraphs
- Using synonym and pronoun referents
- Strength and logic of argument
- Using reporting verbs
- Using connecting language

Topic focus

1 How do each of these make one culture different from another? Brainstorm your ideas with a partner.

- attitudes to time
- religion
- language
- food
- divisions in society
- demography
- health and education
- urbanization
- changes in population size

2 Which of these statements are most similar to you and your culture?

'Religion is a major influence on attitudes and beliefs.'

'Countries that speak the same language as me have the same culture as me.'

'I always follow the clock; being on time is vital for me.'

'Religion has less influence on society today than it used to.'

'Countries that speak the same language as me don't always have the same culture as me.'

'Being late is not important to me; it's more important who I'm with and what is happening.'

3 Look back at the topics and issues you have discussed in Exercises 1 and 2 and think how cultural differences may cause problems in or between societies. In pairs, rank your ideas from most to least important.

Essay structure and organization: structuring paragraphs

Study tip
A paragraph should focus on one topic, and commonly goes from general to specific. There are three main parts to a paragraph: the topic sentence, supporting details and the concluding sentence.

1 a Look at the paragraph below and answer these questions.

    1 What is the main topic of the paragraph?

    2 Which sentence gives you the main topic?

    3 What examples or ideas are used to support this main idea?

    4 What conclusion does the writer reach at the end of the paragraph?

b Match each sentence to one of these functions.

    a topic sentence   **b** supporting sentence(s)   **c** concluding sentence(s)

> Education, one of the most important social institutions, affects all aspects of culture, from economic development to consumer behaviour. The literacy rate of a country is a potent force in economic development. Numerous studies indicate a direct link between the literacy rate of a country and its capability for rapid economic growth. According to the World Bank, no country has been successful economically with less than 50 per cent literacy, but when countries have invested in education, the economic rewards have been substantial. Literacy has a profound effect on marketing. It is much easier to communicate with a literate market than to one which the marketer has to depend on symbols and pictures to communicate.

2 a Read these sentences and answer the questions below.

    a However, this gradual cultural growth does not occur without some resistance; new methods, ideas and products are considered suspect before they are accepted, if ever.

    b A characteristic of human culture is that change occurs.

    c That people's habits, tastes, styles, behaviours and values are not constant but are continually changing can be verified by reading 20-year-old magazines.

    1 What order do you think each of the sentences should go in to form a paragraph?

    2 What is the main topic of the paragraph?

    3 Which sentence gives you the main topic?

    4 What examples or ideas are used to support this main idea?

    5 What conclusion does the writer reach at the end of the paragraph?

b Match each sentence above (a–c) to one of these functions (1–3).

    1 topic sentence   **2** supporting sentence   **3** concluding sentence

3 Underline the main idea and circle the topic in each of these sentences.

    1 Geography exercises a more profound influence than just affecting the sort of jacket you buy.

    2 Family forms and functions vary substantially around the world, even around the country.

    3 Culture is dynamic in nature; it is a living process.

4 Which topic sentence from Exercise 3 are these supporting sentences related to?

  a Indeed, geography (broadly defined here to include climate, topography, flora, fauna and microbiology) has influenced history, technology, economics, our social institutions and yes, our way of thinking.

  b Consider the Dutch executive who lives with his mother, wife and kids in Maastricht in a house that his family has owned for the last 300 years.

  c But the fact that cultural change is constant seems paradoxical, because another important attribute of culture is that it is conservative and resists change.

  d Geographical influences manifest themselves in our deepest cultural values, developed through the millennia.

  e Then there's the common practice of the high-income folks in Cairo buying an apartment house and filling it up with the extended family – grandparents, married siblings, cousins and kids.

  f Or how about the Japanese mother caring for her two children pretty much by herself, often sleeping with them at night, while her husband catches sleep during his four-hour commute.

  g There are a variety of ways societies change. Some have change thrust on them by war or by natural disaster.

  h One view is that culture is the accumulation of a series of the best solutions to problems faced in common by members of a given society.

  i More commonly, change is a result of societies seeking ways to solve the challenges and problems they face.

5 Match these concluding sentences to the topic and supporting sentences from Exercises 3 and 4.

  i All these differences lead directly to differences in how children think and behave.

  ii In other words, culture is the means used in adjusting to the environmental and historical components of history.

  iii The ongoing cultural divide across the English Channel is also representative of geography's historical impact on human affairs.

6 Choose one of these main topics and discuss some possible supporting ideas with a partner.

  1 Companies can have a strong influence on culture.

  2 Media influence a country's culture and values.

  3 Technological developments have a strong influence on cultural change.

7 Write a full paragraph, including concluding sentence, for the topic you brainstormed in Exercise 6.

8 Swap paragraphs with a partner. Assess your partner's paragraph using these questions.

  1 Is there a clear topic? Can you state this in your own words?

  2 Is everything in the paragraph related to the topic?

  3 Do the sentences go from general to specific?

  4 What is the function of the concluding sentence: summarizing the main ideas? leading into the next paragraph? giving the reader something to think about? a combination of these?

Language focus 1: using synonyms and pronoun referents

Study tip
Synonyms and pronoun referents are used to avoid repetition in writing and to link ideas. Recognizing them can help your reading, and using them can add cohesion and variety to your writing.

1 What does the underlined word refer to in each of these sentences?

1 Numerous studies indicate a direct link between the literacy rate of a country and <u>its</u> capability for rapid economic growth.

2 Consider the Dutch executive who lives with <u>his</u> mother, wife and kids in Maastricht in a house that his family has owned for the last 300 years.

3 Then there's the common practice of the high-income folks in Cairo buying an apartment house and filling <u>it</u> up with the extended family – grandparents, married siblings, cousins and kids.

4 Or how about the Japanese mother caring for her two children pretty much by herself, often sleeping with <u>them</u> at night, while her husband catches sleep during his four-hour commute.

Maastricht

2 Complete the sentences below using the pronoun referents in the box.

he	its	their	them	these	this	who

1 Many factors impact on the development of a culture, such as the media, schools, religion and family. _____ factors are some of the most common, no matter which culture is considered.

2 It is important to remember that there is no cultural right or wrong, but that cultures are just different. Every country thinks _____ culture is the best.

3 Cultural boundaries are diminishing. How 'Greek' is the person _____ was born in Athens, educated in London and spent the last 15 years working in the Middle East?

4 It is commonly thought that countries speaking the same language will have similar cultures. _____ misconception can lead to problems if a company uses the same strategy in the USA that it uses in the UK.

5 An individual may borrow many items from another culture and adapt _____ to suit _____ needs.

6 A German businessman working in Switzerland may find that _____ needs to adapt to different working practices to operate effectively.

3 Identify the synonym for each underlined word or phrase in these sentences.

1 The literacy rate of a country is a potent force in economic development. Numerous studies indicate a direct link between the literacy rate of a country and its capability for rapid economic <u>growth</u>.

2 According to the World Bank, no country has been successful economically with less than 50 per cent literacy, but when countries have invested in education, the <u>economic rewards</u> have been substantial.

3 Consider the Dutch executive who lives with his mother, wife and kids in Maastricht in a house that his <u>family</u> has owned for the last 300 years.

4 Complete the sentences below using the synonyms in the box.

ability	aptitude	different	diverse	impact
	influence	quickly	rapid	

1 There was a .... increase in international trade once it became possible to .... transport goods between countries.

2 Cultures can be quite .... , even within the same country. Their .... nature, particularly in large countries, means it is very difficult to define, for example, Brazilian culture.

3 America has had a great .... on world cultures and its .... has been particularly great in the business world.

4 Someone with a natural .... for language may be able to adapt more quickly to a new culture. Language is key to successful adaptation, so linguistic .... should not be underestimated as a tool of adaptation.

5 Complete the paragraph below with synonyms and pronouns referents from the box.

executive	invest	its	managers	spend
	their	these	this	

Many companies today have a global strategy. It is due to **1** .... that many **2** .... choose to **3** .... great sums of money in their marketing campaigns. **4** .... campaigns can make or break a product's success and ultimately a top **5** .... career. Therefore, **6** .... decisions are often based on significant market research, which can require a company to **7** .... vast amounts of money. However, **8** .... success may be dependent on this knowledge.

Evaluating writing: strength and logic of argument

 Arguments should be based on evidence and should also be logical in their nature. It is important to assess both the strength and logic of any argument you produce.

1 Underline the basis on which the conclusion is formed in these statements.

  1 Colours carry different meanings in different countries and as a result, packaging design may vary from country to country.

  2 The concept of time is different in different countries. Punctuality is therefore more likely to be important in some countries than others.

  3 Religion plays a key role in defining many cultures around the world and therefore cannot be separated from other parts of culture.

2 In which of these sentences does the argument follow most logically from its reason?

  a The same language is spoken in the USA as it is in the UK; therefore, the cultures are likely to be similar.

  b The same language is spoken in the USA as it is in the UK; therefore, there are unlikely to be communication difficulties.

  c The same language is spoken in the USA as it is in the UK; therefore, people will buy the same products.

3 a Read this essay question and a sample answer for it, then discuss the questions on page 64 with a partner.

> As the world globalizes, cultures around the world become more similar. Discuss.

Coca-Cola is today sold in over 200 countries of the world and is a sign of the increasing globalization that exists. It is also a clear sign that cultures are becoming similar. This essay will argue that the increase in trade, cheap transport and the increased use of a small group of languages has caused cultures of the world to become similar.

It is possible today to consume products from all around the world without ever having to leave your own country. McDonalds, iPhones, Armani and many more products are available wherever you are in the world. Being able to consume products that represent a culture gives people a greater understanding of the culture. It also means that our lives are gradually becoming similar, no matter where we are.

In the past, people were much less likely to understand another culture, because they had so little contact with cultures other than their own. This limited contact was largely caused by the transportation methods available, resulting in journey times lasting weeks or months instead of hours. Today, it is possible for people to travel to many countries in a short period of time. Many people, myself included, have experienced cultures from not only their region but also from other continents. In my grandparents' generation, few people even went to another city in their home country, let alone for holidays in another country. Being able to take holidays every year in another country is certainly leading to a greater understanding of other cultures.

Although there are some 6,000 languages in the world, there are a small number of languages which dominate world communication. These languages, which include English, Arabic, Spanish, Chinese, Hindi and Urdu, enable people from all around the world to communicate more easily with each other. If a person can speak one of these languages, it is likely that they will be able to converse with anyone, no matter where they are. As we start to speak the same languages, so our cultures will become similar. There are almost no cultural differences between Arabic-speaking countries.

As a result of this increasing trade, cheap transportation and simple communication using a limited number of languages, the cultures of the world are becoming fewer. This process is only likely to continue and will eventually result in one world culture.

1 What weak arguments are there in the first paragraph? Which one do you think is the weakest, and why?

2 Does consuming the products of one country make you understand its culture better?

3 Do you think international brands such as Coca-Cola and McDonalds will sell exactly the same products in every country?

4 Will they promote the product in the same way? What changes might they make, and why?

5 Are all of the languages listed equally useful around the world?

6 How good do you think you need to be in a language to help you understand a country's culture?

7 Could you be fluent in a language without any contact with the language's country of origin?

8 Do all countries speaking the same language have the same culture?

9 Will there ever be one world culture?

b Identify all the arguments in paragraph 3 and rank them in order from most valid to least valid. Discuss your ranking with a partner.

4 Choose the most logical conclusion (a, b or c) for each of these arguments. Discuss your choice with a partner.

1 As economic globalization continues, …
a cultures are likely to become similar.
b large companies are likely to dominate retail markets.
c more people are likely to learn English.

2 English is the world's dominant language …
a and is the reason why more countries are becoming similar to America.
b and is likely to continue to be so for a number of years.
c but has little or no influence on other cultures of the world.

5 With a partner, write a logical conclusion for each of these premises.

1 Families play a key role in shaping a culture, and in many parts of the world, families are changing; …

2 More and more countries conduct business with China …

3 The products we consume are changing …

Using sources: using reporting verbs

1 Underline the reporting verbs in these sentences.

   1 Hofstede (2001) defines five key ways in which cultures differ.

   2 Whilst Hofstede (2001) claimed that there are five main features to a culture, it is perhaps limited to restrict the definition of culture to just five areas.

   3 Hofstede (2001) demonstrated that there are clear differences in power roles between countries.

2 Match these reporting verbs (1–6) to their definitions (a–f).

1 argue	**a** to say something is true without being able to prove it
2 show	**b** to make the truth or existence of something known
3 claim	**c** to give the reasons for your ideas, opinions and beliefs
4 define	**d** to show that something is true
5 explain	**e** to say what the meaning of something is
6 prove	**f** to make something clear or easy to understand by giving more information about it

3 Replace the reporting verb in italics in each of the sentences below with the correct form of a reporting verb from the box that has a similar meaning.

> **assert   demonstrate   describe**

   1 Levy (2009) *defines* culture as a system of shared beliefs.

   2 Schlink (2010) *argues* that culture and language cannot be separated.

   3 Zane (2007) *showed* in his study of leadership styles that there are significant differences in the role of managers throughout the world.

4 How does the different reporting verb convey the writer's intention or opinion in each of these sentences?

   a Nemirovsky (2010) *describes* culture as being influenced by four main areas: religion, family, the media and education.

   b Nemirovsky (2010) *maintains* that culture is influenced by four main areas: religion, family, the media and education.

   c Nemirovsky (2010) *demonstrated* that culture is influenced by four main areas: religion, family, the media and education.

5 Use the notes below to:

   a argue for the topic;   **b** argue against the topic;   **c** state the topic neutrally.

Culture + language = not separate (Sitch, 2010)

Language focus 2: using connecting language

1 Match each of these sentences (1–5) to the method of connection used (a–e).

a related ideas and examples

b sequence

c comparison/contrast

d cause/effect

e problem/solution

1 Less was known about cultures of the world *prior to* the industrial revolution.

2 Many cultural misunderstandings *are due to* learned behaviours that are acceptable in one culture but not in another.

3 The role of family within in society, and *in addition* that of women, can impact significantly on cultural expectations.

4 The main *issue* is the loss of traditional customs.

5 Diets have changed throughout the world; *likewise,* rates of obesity have increased.

2 Put these connecting words and phrases in the correct column of the table below.

accounts for   associated with   conversely   corresponds to   derived from   distinction between   furthermore   moreover   ongoing   stems from   stimulates   subsequent   successive   to overcome   to solve   unlike

related ideas and examples	sequence	comparison/contrast	cause/effect	problem/solution

3 Complete these sentences with a word or phrase from Exercise 2 to show the type of connection you think is most likely.

1 The initial problems were caused by poor communication skills; _____ problems were caused by an unwillingness to be open to new ideas.

2 The culture of a country is very strongly _____ the history of the region.

3 If people are able _____ some of their preconceptions about other cultures, then they are usually much more able to adapt to living in that culture.

4 Punctuality is considered important in the UK; _____ , schedules are second to the event itself in many Mediterranean countries.

5 Many cultural prejudices _____ limited knowledge that is also often very outdated.

4 Write brief paragraphs to show the connection between each of these ideas. Look back through the unit for ideas if you need to.

1 Literacy and economic growth

2 A society where families are central to the culture and one where they are not

Unit extension

1 Choose another culture you think you know well and research similarities to and differences between it and your own culture. Write a brief text describing them.

2 Choose two countries that have strong stereotypes about each other, for example France and the UK. Research the causes of these stereotypes and the effects they have on people. Write a brief text describing them.

3 What problems do you think someone may have adapting to your country's culture? Write a brief text describing them.

8 Personality

Aims

- Paragraph logic
- Writing an effective conclusion
- Writing direct and indirect quotes
- Using noun collocations

Topic focus

1 a Think about two or three different friends or members of your family. Write three or four adjectives to describe each person.

   b Swap lists with a partner and briefly describe the people on your list.

   c Has your partner focused mainly on strengths, weaknesses or both? Try to help your partner develop an equal balance of strengths and weaknesses for each person.

2 a Which of these jobs do you think each person from Exercise 1 would be best at, and why?

   - actor
   - researcher
   - police officer
   - shop assistant

   b Think about each person's weaknesses. What might they find hard about the job you have given them?

Evaluating writing: paragraph logic

 Paragraph logic is an important aspect of writing. It is mainly achieved by ordering the paragraph topics logically and by structuring the information within a paragraph in a coherent way.

1 a **Look at these plans for the order of paragraphs in different types of writing. For each pair, which order do you think is better, and why? Or could both be good, depending on your aims?**

Argument essays	
A 1 Introduction with main line of argument 2 Arguments for + support 3 Arguments against + support 4 Conclusion	**B** 1 Introduction with main line of argument 2 Arguments against + support 3 Arguments for + support 4 Conclusion

Problem/solution essays	
A 1 Introduction highlighting the problem 2 Solution 1 3 Solution 2 4 Solution 3 5 Conclusion	**B** 1 Introduction highlighting the problem 2 Solution 3 Further details on the solution 4 Further details on the solution 5 Conclusion

Comparing/contrasting essays	
A 1 Introduction 2 All parts of the first idea 3 All parts of the second idea, showing similarities and differences 4 Conclusion	**B** 1 Introduction 2 First part of the first idea 3 Comparison/contrast with the first part of the second idea 4 Second part of the first idea 5 Comparison/contrast with the second part of the second idea 6 Conclusion

b **Compare your ideas with a partner and discuss your reasons.**

2 **In each of these paragraphs, underline the sentence you think is not related to the main topic of the paragraph.**

A

> One of the most popular methods of recruiting a candidate for a job on the basis of personality is through psychometric testing. This is a test of personality which shows characteristics of the candidate and enables managers to consider how the person will fit into their existing team. Personality plays a key role in all aspects of our lives. Such testing is controversial, as is much personality testing, such as handwriting analysis. However, it could be argued that the test is grounded within much theoretical literature and provides companies with another useful recruitment tool.

B

Two global terms used to describe people are introvert and extrovert. Extroverts can be defined as people who see the importance of having and developing social skills and are commonly described as outgoing or sociable. Introverts, on the other hand, tend to be more focused on their own mental life. They are commonly described as being reserved, shy or withdrawn, and often struggle in social situations. Introverts and extroverts often have very different roles to play within a company. Stereotypically, people often view introversion and extroversion as being on a continuum, with people being either one or the other. Jung, amongst others, argued that everyone is both introvert and extrovert and that these characteristics fluctuate, depending on the situation the person is in.

3 Put these sentences in the most logical order to form a paragraph. Refer to pages 59–60 for tips and advice if you are not sure.

a He identified a related set of dimensions which he believed more accurately and more comprehensively explained different personalities (Jung, 1923).

b Research conducted in the 1950s and 1960s into the field of management was strongly influenced by Jung's methodology and ideas.

c The work of Carl Jung (1875–1961) is the basis for many working within personality theory.

d The theory or concept was to become known as 'analytical psychology'.

e This approach proved extremely influential in what was to become mainstream teaching in management and organizational behaviour.

f People like Myers-Briggs, Maslow and even McGregor all display influences of Jung's work, however much they have misused or abused his work.

Essay structure and organization: writing an effective conclusion

 The main functions of a conclusion are to summarize the main ideas and to give closing comments or thoughts on these ideas. It also often restates the thesis (the main scope/line of argument) in different words. It may also make reference to the future, but it does not usually include any new information.

1 Complete the missing words in these concluding expressions.

To conclude, …

In conclusion, …

The following c _ _ _ l _ _ _ _ _ s can be d _ d _ _ _ d.[1]

To sum up, …

In s _ _ _ _ r_ , … [2]

To _ u _ _ a _ _ _ _ , … [3]

The main ideas can be s _ _ _ a _ _ _ d thus: … [4]

In brief, …

In s _ _ _ _ , … [5]

2 Rewrite these sentences using expressions from Exercise 1. You may need to change the form of the word.

1 It can be concluded that Jung's work was influential in the development of the study of organizational behaviour and management.

2 In summary, this essay has looked at the effectiveness of psychometric testing and its importance to the modern-day recruitment process.

3 Stated briefly, personality is highly influential in the formation of successful teams.

4 In summary, the key idea is that whilst psychometric testing has its flaws, it can still be a useful recruitment tool.

3 Match these thesis statements (1–4) to their paraphrased equivalent in the conclusions (a–d).

1 The Myers-Biggs theory can provide a method for organizing and classifying behaviour into personality types.

2 People's personality is influenced by both their environment and their genetic make-up.

3 This essay will argue that people are neither wholly extrovert nor introvert, but in fact have potential to be both.

4 It could be argued that management is a set of learned skills, whereas effective leadership is dependent on individual personality.

a Both nature and nurture play a key role in developing an individual's personality.

b Therefore, whilst many consider human behaviour to be random, it can be seen that this concept allows for the systematic grouping of characteristics.

c Managers can therefore be trained, but leaders are born with an innate ability to lead.

d Consequently, depending on the situation, individuals can be both reserved and outgoing or confident and shy.

4 Paraphrase these thesis statements so that you could use them in a conclusion.

1 Personality plays a key role in the effective functioning of a team.

2 Arguably interviews display an individual's personality effectively, and therefore psychometric tests are simply time consuming.

5 a Match this thesis statement to its paraphrase in the conclusion below.

> *This essay will argue that environment and genetics have an equal effect on personality, whether that be to create a leader or a criminal.*

Early studies highlighted the influence of genetics on personality development, with Lombroso famously highlighting body type as a key factor in the development of criminal personalities. Later, twin studies went on to try to separate the influence of nature and nurture. However, neither have been shown to have a dominant influence on the development of individual personalities. As a result, much popular media's interpretation of a person's background impacting on their propensity to cause crime is potentially flawed. Whilst this clearly will have an influence to some extent, it is important to remember that there is also a certain genetic disposition to such acts.

b Find sentences in the conclusion above which represent these functions.

1 logical conclusion

2 summarizes main ideas

3 closing thoughts

Using sources: writing direct and indirect quotes

1 a **Read these two extracts and underline the information that comes from another source in each one.**

A

The Myers-Briggs test of personality is perhaps one of the best-known personality tests. O'Doherty (2007:87) describes it as 'a robust practical tool that enables psychologists to classify and identify people in ways they claim are consistent with the theory worked out by Jung'.

B

Whilst the Myer-Briggs theory is a valuable theory that has fed into further research in the field, there are key weaknesses in the underlying principles. O'Doherty (2007) asserts that theory fails to demonstrate whether personality comes merely from birth and our environment, or is in fact shaped by the decisions we have to make.

b **Tick the information that is included about each source.**

	extract A	extract B
publisher		
author surname		
author first name		
year of publication		
page number		
place of publication		
quotation marks		

2 a **Read this statement and say which of the two pieces of information below you would use to support it, and why.**

   There are a number of factors that are important in shaping our personality.

   a In addition to genetic factors, there is surely a significant amount of social determination that explains personality.

   b We also have a number of ways of classifying personality, from the relatively simple to the more complex.

b **Use the relevant information to directly reference your chosen piece of information from above.**

   a Damien O'Doherty, 2007, page 87, Cengage, London, *Individual differences, personality and self*

   b Damien O'Doherty, 2007, page 76, Cengage, London, *Individual differences, personality and self*

Paraphrasing practice **3 a Read this statement and say which of the two pieces of information below you would use to support it, and why.**

Personality plays a key role in hiring the right person for a role.

a The most important reason managers need to know how to measure personality is that research has shown that personality tests are useful in hiring decisions.

b A number of approaches have been developed to evaluate stress and an individual's ability to handle stress.

b Work with a partner. Close your books. Student A, tell your partner the main idea of (a) above, and Student B, tell your partner the main idea of (b). Write down what your partner tells you.

c Open your books and compare what you wrote. How different is it? If it is still quite similar, think about changing:

- word order
- word formation
- synonyms.

d Underline the other parts you would change and make those changes.

e Use this information to indirectly reference your chosen piece of information.

a page 92, *Organizational Behavior: Global and South African Perspectives*, S.P. Robbins, T.A. Judge, A. Odendaal, G. Roodt, Cape Town, 2009, Pearson

b page 50, *Organizational behavior: Individuals, groups and organizations*, Ian Brooks, Pearson, Harlow, 2009

Language focus: using noun collocations

1 a Underline the verbs and circle the nouns in these sentences.

1 A significant number of jobs require applicants to complete a psychometric test.

2 Human Resources are responsible for the recruitment process of a firm.

3 A particular concern for many managers is the personality of new recruits fitting into the existing team.

b Which sentences above contain these structures?

1 adjective + noun   **2** noun + noun   **3** noun + preposition

> **Study tip**
> Try to learn vocabulary in chunks. Learn pairs of words that commonly go together (*collocations*), not just the noun or verb in isolation.

2 Match these adjectives to the nouns they commonly collocate with. Some collocate with more than one noun. Use a dictionary to help you if necessary.

broader   central   changing   compelling   concrete   conflicting
empirical   equal   ethnic   growing   important   major   minor
overwhelming   particular   positive   prevailing   principal   root
significant   strategic   underlying   wide   widespread

1 evidence   **2** role   **3** interest   **4** aspect   **5** cause   **6** attitude
7 variation   **8** proportion

3 Complete these sentences using the collocations from Exercise 2 in the correct form.

1 The .... cause of her leaving the job was her relationships with her colleagues rather than other lesser causes, such as salary, hours and office space.

2 The idea was largely a hypothesis and lacked the support of any .... evidence based on research.

3 Her .... attitude was apparent in the interview process. Everyone could feel her enthusiasm.

4 His role in parliament and his ownership of a company were considered to be .... interests because his company won a number of government contracts.

5 Although not everyone was interested in the concept, there was certainly .... interest, with a greater number of enquiries.

6 .... proportions of both men and women are hired by the firm.

7 She found the job limiting and wanted something that gave her a .... role with variation in tasks.

8 It is possible that personality could be influenced by .... variation, because arguably environment plays a role in personality development.

4 **Complete the phrases below using the prepositions in the box so that they match the given meanings.**

at	behind	for	in	into	of	on	to

1 look ....   to examine something

2 changes ....   developments

3 insight ....   a clear, deep understanding

4 influence ....   to have an effect on something

5 basis ....   the foundation or root of an idea

6 reason ....   an explanation of why something happens

7 approach ....   the method for doing something

8 rationale ....   reasons or intentions

5 **Complete these sentences using the collocations from Exercise 4.**

1 Both genes and the environment have an .... personality.

2 The .... the Myers-Briggs theory comes from the work of Jung.

3 Many thinkers and experts have been trying to gain an .... human personality ever since Hippocrates' early work.

4 The .... using psychometric testing is often to try to match the personality to the existing team.

5 Employers take a .... a number of factors when hiring someone.

6 .... technology has resulted in teams working virtually, often meaning that personality will be conveyed in writing rather than face-to-face.

7 The .... leaving a company can often be based on personality differences with a manager.

8 One .... understanding personality is to ask people questions to discover their underlying traits.

Unit extension

1 **Research the topic for this essay question and write a 500-word essay. Include an introduction, a conclusion and at least one direct and one indirect reference.**

> Compare and contrast two different personality tests. Evaluate the strengths and weaknesses of each.

2 **Bring your essay to the next class. Work with a partner to evaluate each other's organization, conclusion and integration of sources.**

9 Ethics

- Evaluating solutions
- Writing problem/solution essays
- Verb collocations
- Incorporating quotes
- Active and passive

Topic focus

1 a Rate these actions on a scale of 1 to 10, where 1 is 'totally unacceptable' and 10 is 'totally acceptable'.

1 Giving cash privately to a police officer to avoid paying a larger fine for driving too fast.

2 A government minister accepting money to help a company get a government contract.

3 Giving a gift to a member of another organization that your company has a contract with.

4 Paying money to an individual so that they use their power in a company to get a job done more quickly.

b Share your answers with a partner and explain the reasons for your choice.

2 Which of these opinions do you most agree with? Why?

1 Bribery is sometimes necessary for business.

2 Bribery can help make a business profitable.

3 Bribery is unethical.

4 Bribery is a criminal offence and should be punished.

5 Bribery is simply a way of business life.

6 If people had a good basic income, they would not accept bribes.

3 Look at this essay question. Discuss your initial ideas with a partner.

Suggest and evaluate solutions to the issue of corruption.

Evaluating writing: evaluating solutions

1 a One basic way of evaluating solutions is to rank them in order from best to worst. Look at this problem and discuss your opinion of each of the suggested solutions in groups.

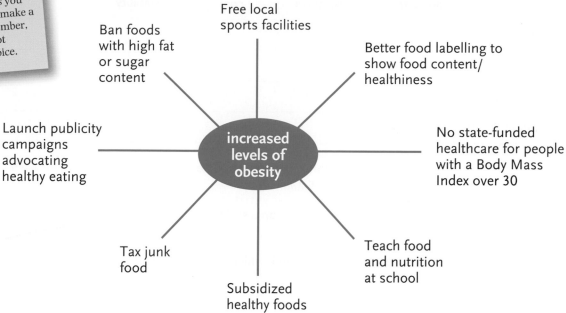

b Rank the solutions from 1 to 8, where 1 is the best solution and 8 is the worst.

c Work with another group. Explain the reasons for your order.

2 a Another method of evaluating solutions is to compare each solution against another. Work in small groups to think of as many solutions as possible to this problem.

Traffic congestion in a large city

b Record your solutions in a table like this.

	solution B	solution C	solution D
solution A			
solution B			
solution C			

c When you compare solution A with solution B which is better? Write your answer in the table, then continue comparing the other solutions.

d How many times was each solution selected? Based on this form of analysis, which is the best solution?

3 a A third method of evaluation scores each solution on different criteria. Work in small groups to think of as many solutions as possible to this problem.

Limited fossil fuels

b Record your solutions and ideas in a table like this.

	long term	short term	cost	viability		
solution A						
solution B						
solution C						
solution D						

c Can you think of any other factors you need to consider for each solution other than those listed?

d Score each factor on a scale of 0–5 for each solution, where 0 = poor and 5 = very good.

e Using this method, which solution is the best?

Essay structure and organization: problem/solution essays

1 Decide whether each of these sentences relates to a problem, a solution or an evaluation. Underline the language that helped you make your selection.

1 Governments could lower taxation on companies to provide support.

2 Corruption causes social, economic and political unrest.

3 This would enable companies to re-invest into the growth and development of their business.

4 However, a cash amount smaller than the electronic fine could still be demanded.

5 Many small companies are going out of business.

6 Fines could be paid via machines rather than cash.

2 With a partner, complete this chart with the solutions you think would be most effective.

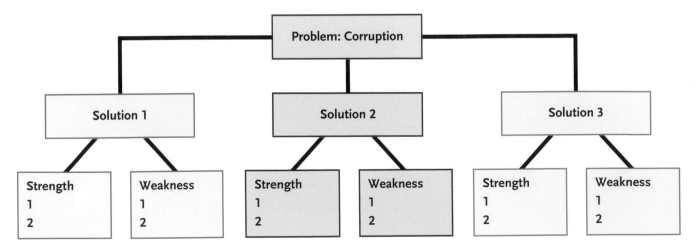

3 Work with another pair and compare your solutions. Can you add any further weaknesses or strengths to each solution?

4 a In Unit 8, you looked at different structures for different types of writing. What were the two suggested structures for problem/solution essays? (See page 68 if you can't remember.)

b When might one structure be better than the other?

5 a Use this quote to help you write a paragraph describing and defining corruption. Make sure your paragraph has a topic sentence, examples and a concluding sentence.

'The abuse of entrusted power for private gain. Corruption can be classified as grand, petty and political, depending on the amounts of money lost and the sector where it occurs.' (Transparency International, 2009:14)

b Swap paragraphs with a partner. Underline the topic sentence, examples and concluding sentence in your partner's paragraph.

6 Choose one of your solutions from Exercise 2 and write a paragraphs describing it.

7 Which of these terms for evaluating solutions relate to weaknesses, and which relate to strengths?

comprehensive   efficient   fallacious   flawed   improve   inadequate
insufficient   lacking   limited   misguided   notable   outmoded
sound   unsuitable   valid

'Oh, I can be reliable, and for an extra three
hundred a week, I can be efficient, too.'

www.CartoonStock.com

8 Write a paragraph that evaluates your suggested solution.

9 Add a suitable conclusion and introduction to your essay. Refer to Units 4 and 8 if you are not sure how to structure them.

Language focus 1: verb collocations

1 Match these verbs (1–5) to the nouns below that they commonly collocate with. A number of collocations are possible for each.

1 discuss   2 examine   3 demonstrate   4 list   5 observe

behaviour   causes   data   effects   features   ideas   issues

2 Complete these sentences with words from Exercise 1.

1 This essay will discuss the .... that caused the most high-profile fraud cases of the 20th century.

2 The report then moves onto examine the .... collected from each step of the experiment.

3 This essay will demonstrate the .... of consumer choice on the ethical behaviour of companies.

4 This essay will start by listing the main .... of unethical behaviour.

5 The long-term aim of the project is to observe the .... of individuals in particular situations.

3 Complete the phrases below using the prepositions in the box so that they match the given meanings.

for	from	from	of	to	to	with	with

1 couple ....   to join or combine

2 emerge ....   to become known, especially after examining or questioning

3 argue ....   to give reasons to support opinions, ideas or beliefs

4 react ....   to behave in a particular way as a result of something else

5 associate ....   to connect to

6 convince ....   to persuade someone or make them certain of something

7 attribute ....   to say that something is the result or work of someone or something else

8 benefit ....   to be helped by someone or something

4 Complete these sentences using the collocations from Exercise 3 in the correct form.

1 In the UK legal system, many new laws .... cases or situations have never been tried before. These can then set a legal precedent.

2 Certain companies' names, such as Enron, have become very strongly .... with the concept of corruption.

3 Their poor financial performance .... the bribery scandal had a negative impact on the company share price.

4 A bribe is mainly used as a way of .... people .... behave in an unethical manner.

5 The way in which a company .... an ethical scandal can have a significant impact on the public's perception of the company.

6 Her political success was .... her ethical and moral behaviour.

7 One main issue with corruption is that individuals .... the situation to the detriment of society.

8 Most people would argue against bribery from a moral point of view, but some companies have .... it in certain cases, arguing that without the payment of bribes in certain countries, it is almost impossible to do business.

Using sources: incorporating quotes

1 a Put these sentences in a logical order to form a paragraph.

    a The countries not willing to invest were those from societies who domestically view corruption as a negative aspect of business; however, those most willing to invest were from countries less concerned about bribery and corruption.

    b A country's reputation for corruption can have a negative impact on attracting foreign investment.

    c Unfortunately, the countries often perceived to be the most corrupt are also those arguably most in need of attracting foreign investment.

    d Simmons and Simmons and Control Risks (2006) found in a survey that a number of respondents would not invest in a country which had a reputation for corruption.

b Compare your answers with a partner and answer these questions.

    1 What is the main aim of the paragraph?

    2 How has the writer used the quote to support the main idea?

2 a Read this paragraph and underline the text from other sources.

Countries, companies and individuals throughout the world are concerned with corruption to varying degrees. Transparency International (2010) claims corruption is the world's most significant problem today. Whilst it could be argued that corruption underlies or feeds into many issues such as war and famine, this

perhaps exaggerates the importance of the issue. However, in certain countries, corruption is considered a lesser concern. Simmons and Simmons and Control Risks (2006) found that in certain countries, corruption is widely accepted, with one respondent from Hong Kong stating that bribery is simply part of business. These wide-ranging perceptions of the significance of corruption reflect the difficulty companies have in operating globally. Not only do perceptions of corruption vary from country to country, but also the way in which countries attempt to deal with the issue also differ greatly.

b Answer these questions.

    1 What is the name of the author in each source?

    2 What is the year of each source?

    3 What verb has been used to introduce the quote?

    4 How does this verb help to indicate the author's opinion of the quote?

    5 How else does the author show their opinion of the quote?

3 Match these indirect quotes (1–3) to the correct comment (a–c).

1 Transparency International (2010) argues that due to the hidden nature of corruption, perception of corruption is the more effective measure.

2 In 2010, on its scale from 10 (very clean) to 0 (highly corrupt), Transparency International found that three-quarters of the 178 countries surveyed scored below 5 in the index.

3 Denmark, New Zealand and Singapore were considered the least corrupt countries, according to Transparency International (2010).

a Highlighting the connection between corruption and economic development, it is interesting to note that of the top ten least corrupt countries from the corruption perception index, seven are also in the top ten of the human development index.

b So whilst the index does not actually show how corrupt a country is, it gives an indication as to the levels of corruption in society.

c … showing quite clearly that corruption is a concern throughout the world.

4 a Look at this thesis statement and two quotes from the main body of the essay. Thinking about the main line of argument, how might the author intended to use each quote?

Whilst corruption is generally associated with the actions of individuals in companies or governments, the impact is largely on the wider society.

1 Hamilton and Webster (2009) argue that governments may make decisions based on who pays the highest bribe rather than on concerns such as price and quality.

2 Financial resources are often taken away from public-service projects and given to projects such as power stations where there is greater chance of bribery occurring (Hamilton and Webster, 2009).

b Write a topic sentence to introduce each quote.

c Write a sentence commenting on each quote in relation to the main line of argument

d Conclude the paragraphs and link the first one to the second one.

e Swap paragraphs with a partner. Check your partner's paragraphs for the following:

- Is the topic sentence clear and everything in the paragraph clearly related to the topic sentence?
- Have they commented on the quote? Is the comment clearly and closely related to the quote?
- Have they drawn an appropriate conclusion based on the evidence provided?

Language focus 2: active and passive

1 **Match these sentences (1–2) to the explanations (a–b).**

1 Worldcom fraudulently claimed to be in profit when it had actually made a loss.

2 Resources are diverted away from important social projects.

a When the subject is not doing the action, we use the passive voice.

b When the subject is completing the action, we use the active voice.

2 **Complete this news report about an ethical scandal with the correct form of the verbs in brackets.**

The impacts of corruption **1** _____ (*feel*) throughout the whole of society, and this wider impact of corruption **2** _____ (*raise*) as an issue during today's talks. Top business and political leaders all **3** _____ (*believe*) that corruption is an issue for the development of society. In particular, it **4** _____ (*suggest*) that corruption has hindered the development of many poorer countries. The leaders of these countries strongly **5** _____ (*dispute*) these claims, pointing to issues such as famine and drought as the underlying causes of the lack of development.

3 **Write sentences in the tenses given in brackets using these prompts. You may need the passive or the active voice.**

1 (past simple) politicians / discuss / corruption

2 (present simple) corruption / consider / a serious issue

3 (present simple) Transparency International / believe / corruption / serious

4 (past simple) Worldcom / find / committing fraud

5 (present simple) fraud / occur / more commonly / poor countries

6 (past simple) Somalia / find / most corrupt country (Transparency International, 2010)

Unit extension

1 **Use the text(s) in the online bank as a source to help you research this essay question.**

Suggest and evaluate solutions to the issue of corruption.

2 **Write a 500-word essay on this topic. Pay particular attention to the overall structure of the essay and your use and incorporation of sources.**

10 Consumer behaviour

- Comparative essays
- Comparing and contrasting
- Writing a bibliography
- Relevance and support

Topic focus

www.CartoonStock.com

1 **When you think of a British or American person, what are the first things that come into your mind?**

2 **Decide whether each of these phrases is stereotypical of Britain or the USA.**

fish and chips   loud   cricket   overweight   baseball   reserved   extravagant
lazy   rich   friendly   polite   patient   patriotic   history   tea   snobbish
bad food   bad weather   formal   social class   cold

3 **Discuss these questions with a partner.**

1 Is there any truth in stereotypes?

2 What is the problem with stereotyping people?

3 Why might companies want to stereotype groups of people?

4 The United Kingdom is often described as a very class-conscious country. Is social class important in your country?

5 How might social class affect consumer behaviour?

Essay structure and organization: comparative essays 1

1 **Read the paragraphs below and answer these questions for each one.**

1 What is the main topic of each paragraph?

2 What example is given to explain each main topic?

3 What things are compared in the paragraph?

4 Underline the comparative language.

5 Is there an implied comparison where comparative language is not used?

A

Warner (1941) identified six social classes: upper upper, lower upper, upper middle, lower middle, upper lower, and lower lower. These classifications imply that access to resources such as money, education and luxury goods increases as you move up the ladder from lower lower to upper upper. For example, in 2006, the richest 20 per cent of US households earned half of all the income. In contrast, the poorest 20 per cent received just over 3 per cent. However, these figures do not tell the whole story, since some poorer families have access to non-taxable income or members may be between jobs, so their income is temporarily low. When you adjust income for other factors and look at the data on a person-by-person basis (while on average 3.1 people live in a household in the top category, only 1.7 live in one in the bottom category), the richest people actually consume four times more than the poorest.

B

A worldwide view is one way to differentiate among social classes. To generalize, the world of the working class (i.e. the lower-middle class) is more intimate and constricted. For example, working-class men are likely to name local sports figures as heroes and are less likely to take long holidays to out-of-the-way places (Durgee, 1986). Immediate needs, such as a new refrigerator or TV, tend to dictate buying behaviour, whereas the higher classes focus on more long-term goals, such as saving for university tuition or retirement (Halliday, 2000). Working-class consumers depend heavily on relatives for emotional support and tend to orient themselves in terms of the local community rather than the world at large. They are more likely to be conservative and family oriented. Maintaining the appearance of one's home and property is a priority, regardless of the size of the house.

2 a **Paragraph B in Exercise 1 describes a 'worldview' of the working class. Discuss these questions with a partner.**

1 Are there clear social classes in your country?

2 If there are, do you think the above description of working classes is true for your country?

b **Decide whether each of these sentences applies to working classes or higher social classes.**

1 Their consumption rate is four times higher.

2 In the US, this group is 20% of the population.

3 In the US, this group has 50% of the wealth.

4 They plan and budget with a long-term strategy.

5 They make purchases for immediate needs.

6 They are concerned about the appearance of their home.

3 **Read this essay question. What ideas could you use from the book so far to help formulate your ideas?**

Compare and contrast the consumer-behaviour patterns of different social classes from a global perspective.

Language focus: comparing and contrasting

1 Complete these sentences with the correct form of the adjectives in brackets.

1 In America, the middle and upper classes have _____ (*few*) children per family.

2 In the United States, Asian immigrants and Asian Americans are _____ (*sensitive*) to brands than other Americans.

3 Due to low costs, Chinese workers earning $14,000 can enjoy stylish clothing, TVs and cell phones. _____ (*wealthy*) Chinese entrepreneurs can enjoy golf lessons, Ferraris and Louis Vuitton clothing.

4 Increased wealth has made shopping a popular leisure pursuit in the Middle East and even arguably the _____ (*popular*) hobby.

5 The class system in the UK was largely based on inherited position; today, it is _____ (*flexible*).

6 The _____ (*big*) emerging markets go by the acronym BRIC: Brazil, Russia, India, China.

2 Look back at the paragraphs on page 83 and at the comparison phrases you underlined. Do they highlight similarities or differences?

3 Put these comparison words and phrases in the correct column of the table below, according to whether they signal a similarity or a difference. Then add the words and expressions from Exercise 2.

the same … as   like   different from   similar to   instead   conversely
on the contrary   on the other hand   however   in the same way   likewise

similarlty	difference

4 Complete the sentences below with expressions from the box.

both	different from	however	in contrast	like
	the same … as	similar to	similarities	

1 _____ to Japan, where many women work, a great deal fewer Arab women work.

2 _____ China and Japan are very brand-conscious societies.

3 Traditionally, English society was based on inherited social-class positions; _____ today, this has faded in part due to the rise in newly wealthy people from working-class backgrounds, such as Sir Alan Sugar and Sir Richard Branson.

4 _____ China, India has had a booming economy in recent years.

5 The Future 7 countries – Argentina, Mexico, Turkey, Egypt, South Africa, Vietnam and Indonesia – are considered _____ today _____ Brazil, Russia, India and China were a number of years ago. People believe these economies have the potential to grow significantly.

6 The upper classes are _____ the working class in the UK, in that both are brand conscious.

7 There are _____ in the way people judge their 'worth' throughout the world, and one method is occupational prestige.

8 Countries as _____ each other as Brazil, Ghana, Japan and Turkey all consider occupation as one method of judging someone's class.

5 a Read this information about the UK. With a partner, think of similarities and differences between the UK and your country.

The UK

It has a service economy.
It has a royal family.
It consists of four countries: England, Northern Ireland, Scotland and Wales.
It is less important today than it was 200 years ago.
It has the world's global language.
It was created in 1801.
It has rain all year round.
It imports more oil than it produces.
It has a strong class system.

b Add any further similarities or differences you know to your lists.

c Write sentence using the expressions from this section to compare and contrast your country with the UK.

Essay structure and organization: comparative essays 2

Method A Block organization	Method B Point-by-point organization
This method groups all point of comparison together, and then all points of contrast together. For example: ● Topic sentence ● All points of comparison ● All points of contrast ● Concluding sentence	This method compares and contrasts each point in turn. For example: ● Topic sentence ● Point of comparison + contrast 1 ● Point of comparison + contrast 2 ● Point of comparison + contrast 3 ● Concluding sentence

1 a Look at the two main methods for organizing a comparative paragraph above. Then look at the sentences you wrote in Exercise 5 above comparing your country and the UK. Which method do you think would be best for organizing a comparative paragraph about them, and why?

b Expand your sentences into a complete paragraph using one of the methods of organization.

2 a The same overall organizational method can be used for the essay as a whole. Read again at the essay question you looked at earlier again (see below) and think about what you know on this topic already from the discussions, paragraphs and brainstorming. Which method do you think you might use?

> Compare and contrast the consumer behaviour patterns of different social classes from a global perspective.

b Think about the research you would need to do to complete this essay. With a partner, write a list of research questions on the topic.

Examples: How is consumer behaviour defined?
How is social class defined?

Using sources: writing a bibliography

 There are a number of different methods of referencing and creating a bibliography. This book focuses on the Harvard system, but always check with a tutor which system you are expected to use.

1 a **Discuss these questions with a partner.**

    1 What is a bibliography, and where do you find it in an essay?

    2 What information do you include in a bibliography?

  b **Think about both the reader and the writer. List reasons why a bibliography is useful.**

Example: for future research

2 **Read this box, then use the information on page 87 to write correct bibliographic entries.**

 Referencing

You will often need to reference a wide range of material for inclusion in bibliographies. Here, we will look at how to reference a book, a contribution to an edited book, a journal article and web pages.

- **Reference to a book**
  Author's surname, INITIALS, year of publication. *Title*. Edition (if not the first). Place of publication: Publisher.

  Example: Soloman, M.R., 2011. *Consumer behaviour: Buying, having and being*. 9th ed. New Jersey: Pearson.

- **Reference to a contribution to an edited book**
  Contributing author's surname, INITIALS, year of publication. Title of contribution. *In*: surname, INITIALS of author or editor of publication followed by 'ed.' or 'eds.' *Title of book*. Place of publication: Publisher, page number(s) of contribution.

  Example: Mahoney, J., 1994. How to be ethical: Ethics resource management. *In*: Harvey, B., ed. *Business ethics: A European approach*. Hemel Hempstead: Prentice Hall, 32–55.

- **Reference to an article in a journal**
  Author's surname, INITIALS, year of publication. Title of article. *Title of journal*, Volume number and (part number), page number(s) of article.

  Example: Swan, M., 2010. Striking a balance. *English Teaching Professional*. 70. 4–6

- **Reference to a website**
  Author's surname, INITIALS (*use the name of the organization if this is not available*), Year. *Title of the article*. Available at: *URL*. (Accessed date)

  Example: Human Development Reports, 2010. *Worldwide trends in the human development index 1980–2010*. Available at: http://hdr.undp.org/en/data/trends/1980-2010/ [Accessed 11 May 2011]

1 David Boddy / *Management: an Introduction* / fourth edition / Prentice Hall / 2007 / Harlow

2 Contribution: Luk Bouckaert / 1994 / Business and community / 154–189
Publication: Brian Harvey / 1994 / *Business Ethics: A European approach* / Hemel Hempstead / Prentice Hall

3 James Venema / 2010 / 12–13
Article title: 'Active word power'
Journal title: *English Teaching Professional*, 69

4 Transparency International / 2010 /
http://www.transparency.org/policy_research/surveys_indices/cpi/2010/results /
Accessed 11 May 2011 / Corruption perceptions index 2010 results.

3 Complete the sentences below using the expressions in the box.

a and *b*	alphabetical order	date order	n.d.

1 When there is no date given, write ⎯⎯⎯⎯⎯⎯ .

2 The whole bibliography should go in ⎯⎯⎯⎯⎯⎯ .

3 When there are two books by the same author from different years, place them in ⎯⎯⎯⎯⎯⎯ . If they are the same year, add the letters ⎯⎯⎯⎯⎯⎯ after each one.

Evaluating writing: relevance and support

> Compare and contrast the consumer-behaviour patterns of different social classes from a global perspective.

1 Read the essay below and on page 88 written in answer to the above question. Analyze how the writer has supported their main arguments by:

- underling examples
- circling explanations
- highlighting any further details.

2 Discuss these questions with a partner.

1 Are all the examples relevant?

2 In what ways are some points not relevant?

Modern life, especially in the developed world, is heavily influenced by the desire to consume. The extent to which consumption rules modern-day life has even lead to the introduction to the English language of the word *affluenza*, which equates the desire and need to continuously consume to the point of debt and the subsequent stress to that of an illness. However, what exactly is consumer behaviour, and how does this behaviour differ from person to person or group to group? Consumer behaviour can be defined as the selection, purchase, usage and disposal of products, services or ideas, and the steps involved in making these decisions. Whether it is by individuals or groups, the ultimate aim is to satisfy a need or desire (Soloman, 2011). Consumers can be segmented into groups in a number of ways, such as age, gender and ethnicity. This essay will compare and contrast consumer-behaviour patterns in terms of social classes.

Segmentation is key in marketing, as it allows consumers to be targeted in a more efficient way. Some, such as Treguer (2002), argue that age is the most effective segmentation criteria, but social class can also be an effective method for targeting consumers. All societies have some form of social hierarchy that recognizes the differing status of individuals within a society (Hoyer and MacInnis, 2009). Largely speaking, the majority of societies can be divided into three distinct classes: the lower, middle and upper classes. America has seven distinct classes, but how are these classes similar or different in their consumer behaviour?

According to Hoyer and MacInnis (2009), the upper classes have the most similarities throughout the world, largely because they have a more international outlook. For example, they can afford to go on holidays to a number of different countries. In contrast, working-class communities around the world tend to be orientated towards their local community (Soloman, 2011). As a result, they can be more reliant on their community for their own identity and therefore more culturally bound in their behaviour. A working-class person in Barcelona is unlikely to support Manchester United. These similarities and differences have important consequences for marketers.

Importantly for marketers, social class in most societies is related in part to income and in particular to how this income is spent. Upper classes tend to have a more long-term, strategic approach to consumption than lower classes (Halliday, 2000), for example the need to repair a car or buy a new phone for the working classes in comparison to saving to buy a house or invest in a pension fund for the higher classes. These consumption patterns will also vary with age, with General Motors successfully targeting consumers with different cars at different stages of their life, but also with different levels of income (Treguer, 2002). Consequently, age and social class cannot be clearly separated.

In conclusion, consumer behaviours differ by segmentation in a number of ways. In general, upper classes around the world are likely to have similar consumption patterns due to their more international long-term outlook. Additionally, working-class consumers are also likely to have similar consumption patterns related to more immediate needs; however, their decisions and behaviour maybe more culturally bound.

Unit extension

1 Use the text(s) provided on the website (www.deltapublishing.co.uk/resources) to help you answer the essay question in this unit.

2 Try to complete further research to support your ideas.

3 Pay particular attention to your method of organization, use of comparative language and accuracy of the bibliography.

11 Nutrition

Aims

- Using language for cause and effect
- Overgeneralizations
- Cause-and-effect essays
- Introduction to extended writing
- Describing trends

Topic focus

1 Read these statements and discuss the questions below with a partner.

> There are over seven billion people in the world.

> There are over one billion people in the world who are overweight.

> There are approximately 800 million people in the world who are malnourished.

1 Which of the above statements do you think is the biggest worry? Why?

2 For each one, can you think of two possible causes and two possible effects?

2 Work with another pair and share your ideas. Separate your causes for each one into main causes to minor causes and decide who is affected in each case.

Language focus 1: cause and effect

Study tip
There are a number of common connectives that signal a cause-and-effect relationship.

1 Circle the cause and underline the effect(s) in each of these sentences.

1 In many countries, the change in diet from cereals to animal products and vegetable oils, accompanied by a decline in physical work, more motorized transport and more television viewing, has caused increases in obesity.

2 A lack of technology, resources or farming skills can lead to food shortages.

3 Better sanitation has resulted in fewer diseases being spread.

2 a Match the two halves of these sentences to form cause-and-effect relationships.

1 Salt, sugar and saturated fats are the ingredients that *contribute to*

2 In 1991, California introduced a snack-food tax that *led to*

3 Scientists investigating changes in food consumption in UK men found that an increase in food intake over the 15-year period studied *accounted for*

4 In many Western countries, junk food is cheap, and *as a result*

5 In many poor countries, junk food is relatively expensive and *consequently*

6 As countries become only slightly wealthier, cheap junk food and less physical work means that people become unhealthier, and *the result is*

a a 10% drop in the sales of such products.

b is likely to be consumed by rich sections of the population.

c most diet-related health problems.

d it is consumed in significant proportions by less affluent people.

e the rapid spread of heart disease, diabetes, respiratory diseases and cancers.

f a 4.7kg (10.4lb) increase in the average male's weight.

b Which of the expressions in *italics* in Exercise 2a show causes, and which show effects?

3 Complete the sentences below using the expressions in the box.

as	cause of	on account of	one effect	result in	thus

1 High levels of salt consumption can .... increases in blood pressure.

2 Less physical activity is one .... the increases in obesity.

3 Obesity levels are now dangerously high in many countries; ...., there is great pressure on many healthcare systems.

4 There are demands to increase the cost of certain food products .... the fact that they are strongly linked to increases in obesity.

5 .... lifestyles have become more sedentary, people's weight has steadily increased.

6 .... of increased wealth in the developing world is the increased levels of obesity.

4 Which of these alternative connectives could you use in each of the sentences in Exercise 3?

because of   cause   hence   one consequence   reason for   since

5 Look at your cause-and-effect ideas from page 89. Write complete sentences using the expressions on this page. Try to use a different connective each time.

Evaluating writing: overgeneralizations

 It is important not to overgeneralize from data or research. You need to analyze and think about exactly who the data is applicable to and in what contexts, and to not claim something is true in all cases when it may not be.

1 a Look at these statements and identify what the weaknesses in them might be.

1 High calorie intake leads to obesity.

2 Body fat is bad for you.

3 Low income is a direct cause of obesity.

4 People with a high metabolism are less likely to be obese.

5 Being fat is worse for your health than being thin.

6 You cannot be overweight and healthy.

b With a partner, add a qualification to each of the claims above.

Example: **1** High calorie intake may lead to obesity, depending on the type of food you are eating and the amount of energy you are expending.

2 Match each of these criticisms (a–f) to the relevant statement (1–6) in Exercise 1.

'The other foot also, Mrs Zipsky!'

a Excessive body fat is bad for you, but humans need a certain amount of body fat to maintain life.

b Correlations do not necessarily mean there is a cause, but non-correlations mean it is difficult to prove a link. There is a non-correlation between resting metabolic rates and weight gain.

c Whilst a high BMI* does correlate with health-related illnesses, so does a low BMI; furthermore, other factors such as genetics need to be considered.

d Food intake alone is unlikely to be the cause of obesity; other factors, such as environmental factors, physical activity and genetics, play a part.

e In the developed world, low income often strongly correlates with high levels of obesity; however, in the developing world, the reverse can be true.

f Low weight levels also have a strong correlation with mortality.

* BMI = Body Mass Index (a calculation based on a person's height and weight that gives an indication of obesity)

3 Discuss these questions with a partner.

1 Why do you think it is easy to make an overgeneralization?

2 What are the consequences of overgeneralizations in academic writing?

3 How can overgeneralizations be avoided?

Essay structure and organization: cause-and-effect essays

1 **Read this essay question, then, with a partner, underline its key sections.**

> Obesity is likely to be the biggest primary healthcare concern in the coming years. Discuss the primary causes of obesity and the effects it has on individual health and the wider society.

2 **Look at this mind map from a student's brainstorming of the essay question in Exercise 1. With a partner, try to add more ideas.**

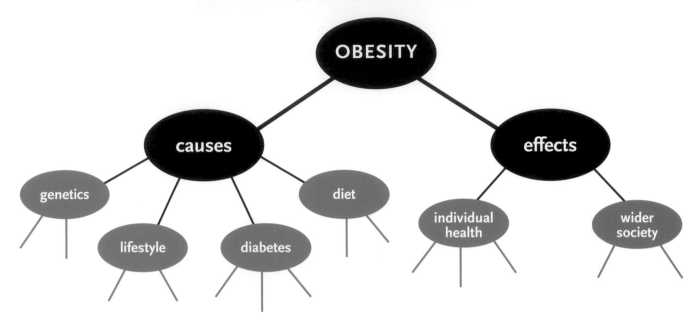

3 **Match the causes (1–3) to the effects (a–c) that will together form the basis the main body of the essay.**

1 The cost of junk food is *leading to*

2 *One reason* for the increase in obesity

3 Obesity is *caused by*

a differing issues in the developing and developed world.

b a range of factors with no one factor, such as a genetic disposition, likely to be solely responsible.

c is the increasingly sedentary lifestyles people lead.

4 **Look again at the cause-and-effect sentences in Exercise 3. Which of these sentences do you think is the most likely thesis statement for the essay?**

a This essay will argue that changes in diet are the sole cause of the increases in obesity.

b This essay will argue that increasingly sedentary lifestyles are the primary cause of obesity.

c A number of factors have played a role in the increasing levels of obesity, and no one factor should be individually blamed.

5 **Match the cause-and-effect sentences from Exercise 3 to these main topics for each paragraph in the essay.**

  i One of the main factors commonly cited as the primary cause of obesity is the changes in dietary habits.

  ii The second most commonly cited factor is the changes in levels of physical activity in modern society.

  iii A number of studies have tried to establish whether there is an innate biological link to the problem of obesity.

Paraphrasing practice 6 a **Which paragraph of the essay would you use these quotes in?**

  1 Both genes and everyday life environmental factors, such as cultural and social mediated food intake and reduced domestic and living work activities, are involved in the obesity pandemia. (Marti et al., 2004)

  2 In 2000, the average man in the UK consumed more food than an equivalent man in 1986. It was found that the difference was enough to make an individual 4.7kg heavier, but in fact the difference is actually 7.7kg. This difference was attributed to the fact there has also been an increase in inactivity in this time (Scarborough et al., 2010).

  3 The relationship between obesity and socio-economic status (SES) varied across countries. Higher SES subjects were more likely to be obese in China and Russia, but in the US, low-SES groups were at a higher risk. (Wang, 2001)

  b **Read the quotes again. Then close your books and try to write down a paraphrase of each quote.**

  c **Compare your answers with a partner.**

7 **Use the ideas you have developed in this unit to write an essay on this question.**

Using sources: introduction to extended writing

 There are a number of challenges associated with extended writing. This section will give you a brief introduction to some of them, and to some skills you can apply to help you overcome them.

1 **One of the most common forms of extended writing in higher education is a dissertation, or thesis. Work in small groups and complete these mind maps.**

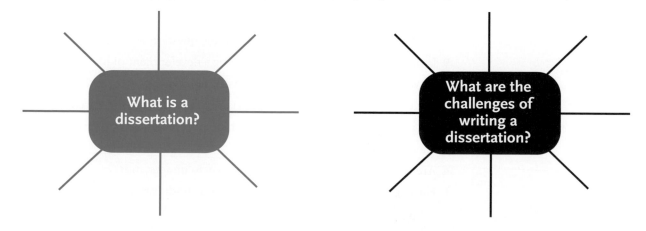

2 Answer these questions.

1 What is the longest piece of academic writing you have had to complete?

2 What is the highest number of sources you have ever used in one piece of academic writing?

3 What are the challenges of including a wide range of sources in your work?
   Example: Seeing connections between theories, ideas and texts

3 Complete the advice below for approaching extended writing using phrases from the box.

feasible	independently	literature	management
	methods	primary	

Time **1** _____ is important in all academic study, but even more so when undertaking a piece of work such as a thesis or dissertation. Many programmes have training in research **2** _____ , but after this, extended writing projects are often conducted largely **3** _____ with tutorial support from a course tutor. Often you will have the freedom to choose your own topic, so it is important to consider whether the topic is **4** _____ – is it manageable in terms of both time and the word count? – and to have a clear standpoint or thesis that you will investigate. Prior to conducting **5** _____ research, you will normally be expected to conduct secondary research into the area in order to become more expert in the field. In some cases, it is possible to base the entire dissertation on secondary research. This section of a dissertation is commonly called a **6** _____ review and commonly follows on from the introduction. The other main sections of a dissertation are typically the methodology, findings and conclusion.

4 Match each of these questions you can ask yourself when approaching extended writing (1–15) to one of these sections (a–d).

a Dissertation focus   **b** Literature review   **c** Methodology   **d** Findings

1 Have you researched seminal, recent and relevant sources?

2 Have you described your methods clearly enough so that someone else could follow the same methodology?

3 Does it look into interesting or important themes from your studies?

4 How have you assessed the quality of the sources you have used?

5 Is the topic clearly defined?

6 Have you made overgeneralizations from your findings?

7 Is the topic of relevance and interest?

8 Have you related your findings back to the question well?

9 Is the literature well connected, showing a development of ideas?

10 Have you shown the significance of your findings?

11 Have you selected the most appropriate method for your research aims?

12 Do you criticize and evaluate current ideas and themes?

13 Have you found enough evidence?

14 Are your findings clearly written and easy to understand?

15 Have you explained the importance of your findings?

5 Based on what you have read in Exercises 3 and 4, what key tips would you give for extended writing?

Example: It must be clearly focused.

Language focus 2: describing trends

1 **Choose the most appropriate word to describe the image below.**

It can be seen from the *chart / diagram / table / graph / figures / statistics* that …

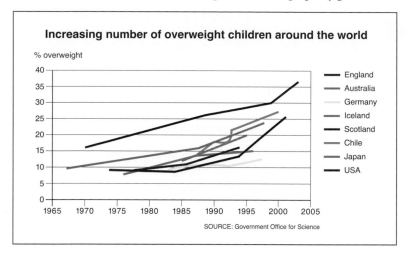

Increasing number of overweight children around the world

% overweight

Legend: England, Australia, Germany, Iceland, Scotland, Chile, Japan, USA

SOURCE: Government Office for Science

2 a **Put the words in the correct order to create other phrases for introducing visuals.**

   1 from / the / as / concluded / can / be / chart, / …

   2 Chart 1, / to / according / …

   3 concluded / that / from / the / chart / be / it / can / …

  b **Which words in the above sentences could be replaced by these expressions?**

   1 diagram/table/graph/figure/data/information

   2 inferred/seen

3 **Look at the line for each country in the graph in Exercise 1 and describe the changes using these words.**

dramatic   gradual   marked   sharp   slight   small   steady   sudden

Example: In the USA, there was a gradual increase in the levels of overweight children between 1970 and 2000, and this was followed by a sharp increase between 2000 and 2003.

4 **How and where could you use this graph in the essay you wrote earlier in the unit?**

Unit extension

1 **Earlier in this unit, you looked briefly at the topics of over-population and malnourishment. Use these ideas as a platform to answer one of these essay questions.**

> Over-population of the world is of less concern than increased urbanization. Discuss.

> Suggest and evaluate solutions to the problem of malnutrition.

2 **Find evidence to support your ideas and try to incorporate the cause-and-effect language you have studied in this unit.**

12 Revision

Essay structure and organization

Paragraph structure (Unit 7)

1 a Put these sentences in the correct order to form a coherant paragraph.

   a For example, car ownership and mass urbanization in China have led to the situation where the Beijing Transportation Research Center (2010) forecast that by 2015, Beijing's average driving speed would be below 15 kilometers an hour.

   b The increasing wealth and population in some countries is placing extreme environmental pressure on a number of societies.

   c This, amongst other factors, has contributed to Beijing being one of the top 20 most polluted cities in the world (World Bank, 2004).

   d Whilst there are inevitable short-term impacts on a city, its economy and its people, one of the most important long-term outcomes is the negative effect this situation will have on people's lives.

   b Answer these questions about the paragraph above.

   1 What is the main topic of the paragraph?

   2 Which sentence gives you the main topic?

   3 What examples or ideas are used to support this main idea?

   4 What conclusion does the writer reach at the end of the paragraph?

   c Match each sentence above (a–d) to one of these functions (1–3).

   1 topic sentence   2 supporting sentence(s)   3 concluding sentence

2 Choose one of these main topics and discuss some possible supporting ideas with a partner.

   a The links between increasing urbanization and obesity

   b Corruption is normal in business.

   c Social class influences consumer behaviour.

3 Write a full paragraph, including a concluding sentence, for the topic you brainstormed in Exercise 2.

Writing an effective conclusion (Unit 8)

4 Find a paraphase for this thesis statement in the conclusion below.

This essay will argue that whilst different countries have differing social class systems, the impact on consumer behaviour is largely the same throughout the world.

As can be seen from the above analysis, in certain countries the class system plays a very strong role in shaping a society and less so in others. However, even when the system is not very strong, there is still a clear influence on consumer behaviour. In particular, the higher and lower classes throughout all societies tend to have very similar purchasing patterns. Broadly speaking, lower classes are more concerned with meeting everyday needs and demands, whereas higher classes take a more long-term strategic approach to consumption. Therefore whilst the marketing message and product might need to be adapted to fit the local needs, the behaviour is largely similar.

5 Match each of the other sentences in the conclusion in Exercise 4 to one of these functions.

1 logical conclusion

2 summarizes main ideas

3 closing thoughts

Problem/solution essays (Unit 9)

6 Decide which of these three categories (a–c) the sentences below relate to.

a problem   **b** solution   **c** evaluation

1 Governments could move public jobs to areas with high unemployment.

2 Urbanization causes social, economic and political unrest.

3 This would allow people to gain employment without moving to overpopulated areas.

4 Whilst there are clear weaknesses, a psychometric test can provide another possible recruitment tool.

5 Many companies find it difficult to recruit staff with the right personality to match their team.

6 Interviewing people in groups could allow for people's personality to become more obvious.

7 Decide which of these sentences describe weaknesses and which describe strengths.

1 In a comprehensive study, Watson (2010) highlights three common causes of malnourishment in the developed world.

2 The study used a limited sample size and, as a result, has limited transferability to other contexts.

3 Insufficient evidence was gathered to support the hypothesis.

4 The study was fundamental in developing modern understanding of dietary requirements.

Comparative essays (Unit 10)

8 a Look at the paragraph below and decide what things are being compared.

b Underline the comparative language.

Countries, companies and individuals throughout the world are concerned with corruption to varying degrees. Transparency International (2010) claims corruption is the world's most significant problem today. Whilst it could be argued that corruption underlies or feeds into many issues such as war and famine, this perhaps exaggerates the importance of the issue. However, in certain countries, corruption is considered a lesser concern. Simmons and Simmons and Control Risks (2006) found that in certain countries, corruption is widely accepted, with one respondent from Hong Kong stating that bribery is simply part of business. These wide-ranging perceptions of the significance of corruption reflect the difficulty companies have in operating globally. Not only do perceptions of corruption vary from country to country, but also the way in which countries attempt to deal with the issue also differ greatly.

9 a Use this information to write a comparative paragraph.

- 1920s in UK: 100,000 crimes recorded
- 1992: 5.6 million crimes recorded in UK
- 2005: lowest level of crime in UK for 20 years
- Today: more people worried about crime

b Swap paragraphs with a partner. Have they used block or point-by-point structure?

Cause-and-effect essays (Unit 11) **10 Exchange the essay that you wrote in Unit 11 with a partner and answer these questions.**

1 Has your partner used expressions showing cause and effect? Underline them.

2 How strong do you think the cause-and-effect claims are that your partner has made?

3 Has your partner provided strong evidence to support the cause-and-effect claims made?

4 What weaknesses are there in any of the cause-and-effect claims?

Using sources

Reporting verbs (Unit 7) **1 Read the paragraph below and think about the writer's stance. Then complete each gap in the paragraph with the most appropriate reporting verb from the box in the correct form.**

argue	define	show

Culture can be **1** _____ as a system of shared beliefs and values. In a globalizing world, it has been **2** _____ that this system is becoming more universal and that a single world culture is developing (Dawkins, 2010). Essentially, the vast cultural differences that once existed are no longer so apparent. However, whilst this may be the case when comparing countries that are geographically similar and at a similar stage of economic development, it is unlikely that this is a universal process. Green (2008) has **3** _____ in a recent study that distinct cultural areas of the world, not limited to country boundaries, are in fact developing. They are, however, still very limited in the area they cover and are a long way from becoming a single global culture of the world.

Direct and indirect quotes (Unit 8) **2 a Which of the two pieces of information below would you use to support this statement, and why?**

Levels of poverty play a key role in the prevalence of corruption.

a Corruption not only reduces the net income of the poor but also wrecks programmes related to their basic needs, from sanitation to education to healthcare. It results in the misallocation of resources to the detriment of poverty-reduction programmes.

b Perceptions are used because corruption – whether frequency or amount – is to a great extent a hidden activity that is difficult to measure.

b With a partner, close your books. Write down what your partner tells you.

Student A: Tell Student B the main idea of information (a) above.

Student B: Tell Student A the main idea of information (b) above.

c Compare what you wrote down with the book. How different is it? If it is still quite similar, think about changing:

● word order

● word formation

● synonyms

d Underline the other parts you would change and make those changes.

e Use this information below to indirectly reference your chosen quote from above.

Transparency International, 2010, www.Transparency.org, accessed 30.07.2011

3 a **Look at this thesis statement and the quotes below from the main body, and think about the main line of argument. How might the author intend to use each quote?**

Whilst obesity is often thought of as a consequence of individual's actions and behaviours, this essay will argue that it is the wider society as a whole that is to blame.

1 At the end of the second millennium, the influence of the individualizing and moralizing discourse of individual responsibility was already waning (Swierstra and Keulartz, 2010).

2 According to the Foresight Programme (2007), obesity is an inevitable result of a society in which high energy consumption, cheap foods, motorized transport and non-physical work are common.

b **Write a topic sentence to introduce each quote.**

c **Write a sentence commenting on each quote in relation to the main line of argument.**

d **Conclude the paragraphs and, in the case of the first, link it to the second one.**

Writing a bibliography (Unit 10)

4 **Use this information to compile a bibliography that includes a book, an edited book, a journal and a website.**

a Wayne Hoyer and Deborah MacInnis / 5th edition / 2010 / Mason / Cengage Publishing / Consumer behaviour

b contribution: Private troubles, public issues / 2010 / C. Wright-Mills / pages 5–8 publication: Anthony Giddens and Philip Sutton / Sociology: introductory readings / Polity Press / 3rd edition / Cambridge / 2010

c Cathy Cobb and Wayne Hoyer / 1986 / pages 384–409 / Planned vs impulse purchase behaviour / Journal of retailing, 64(4)

d Dan Fost / New York Times / 2008 / available at http://www.nytimes.com/2008/02/25/technology/25satisfaction.html / accessed 30 July 2011 / On the Internet, everyone can hear your complaint

Evaluating writing

For this section, you will need a copy of your essay from Unit 11 or another unit. Either using your own essay or that of a partner, evaluate it using these questions.

Line of argument (Unit 7)

1 What is the main argument in the essay?

2 Underline the part in each paragraph that refers back to the main argument.

3 If there is no connection to the main argument, what is the function of the paragraph? Does a link need to be added?

4 Have both sides of the argument been presented?

Paragraph logic (Unit 8)

5 Look at each paragraph and, in a few words, summarize the main topic.

6 Does the topic sentence state this main topic clearly?

7 Is everything related to the main topic?

8 Does the paragraph either have a conclusion or make a transition to the next paragraph?

Evaluating solutions (Unit 9)

9 Does the essay you have chosen require solutions?

If so, does it:

10 ... evaluate each of these solutions?

11 ... give evidence and examples in evaluating the solution?

12 ... consider alternative solutions carefully and in a balanced manner?

Relevance and support (Unit 10)

13 What method of support has been chosen?

14 Why were the supporting examples, details or explanations selected?

15 Are there any weaknesses in the support chosen, for example bias, sample size, overgeneralization, relevance?

Overgeneralizations (Unit 11)

16 Has evidence been used to provide specific support that does not overgeneralize?

17 Have any of the quotes or studies selected overgeneralized?

Comparing and contrasting (Unit 10)

9 Match the two halves of these sentences. Pay attention to the comparative expressions used.

1 Language is one factor that makes one culture *different from*

2 It is commonly thought that when one country speaks *the same* language *as*

3 Monochronic countries are those in which events strictly follow the clock. *Conversely,*

4 *Like* Germany,

a another one, then the cultures will be similar.

b another one.

c England is a monochronic culture.

d polychronic cultures focus more on the event that is happening rather than the time frame it is happening in.

Cause and effect (Unit 11)

10 Match the two halves of these sentences to form cause-and-effect relationships.

1 Low literacy rates can *contribute to*

2 Some argue that the spread of English has *led to*

3 International travel *accounts for*

4 Many jobs and lifestyles in the developed world are quite sedentary, and *as a result*

5 Introvert and extrovert traits are not fixed, and *consequently,*

6 Poverty and corruption are interlinked, and *the result can be*

a the extinction of minority languages.

b people are burning less energy.

c a country's poor economic growth.

d people may be perceived differently, depending on the context.

e that in areas that should receive financial aid, not all of the money reaches the intended target.

f a large proportion of most people's carbon footprint.

11 Write sentences on these topics that express a cause-and-effect relationship.

1 overpopulation 2 increased urbanization 3 increased consumption

Describing trends (Unit 11)

12 Write a brief paragraph describing the changes in population growth in the developed and developing regions of the world, using data shown in this graph.

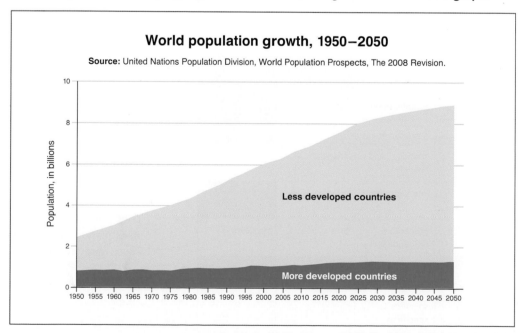

World population growth, 1950–2050

Source: United Nations Population Division, World Population Prospects, The 2008 Revision.

Population, in billions

Less developed countries

More developed countries

1950 1955 1960 1965 1970 1975 1980 1985 1990 1995 2000 2005 2010 2015 2020 2025 2030 2035 2040 2045 2050

Academic Word List exercises

Sub-list 1

The words in these exercises all come from Sub-list 1 of the AWL.

1 Match the words (1–10) to their definitions (a–j).

1 concept
2 derive
3 establish
4 estimate
5 financials
6 interpretation
7 policy
8 procedure
9 require
10 specific

a to start something, such as a company
b relating to money
c actions that are the accepted way of doing things
d an idea or principle
e an opinion or explanation of what something means
f to need
g a official plan or ideas for a particular situation agreed by a group, organization or government
h related to one particular thing
i to come from something
j to guess something such as a value

 Some words in Exercise 1 have multiple meanings. It is important to use the context and, if necessary, a dictionary to help you check the meaning when you are uncertain.

2 Complete this table with the different forms of words from Exercise 1.

verb	noun	adjective	adverb
conceptualize	concept conception conceptuali-zation	1	conceptually
derive	2 .... derivative		
3	establishment	established	
estimate	4	estimated	
finance	finance financier	financial	5 ....
6	interpretation	interpretative interpretive	
7	procedure proceedings	8	procedurally
require	9		
specify	specification specifics specificity	specific	10 ....

3 Complete each of these sentences with the word in brackets in the correct form.

1 The .... (*conceptualize*) of the test was to test students' understanding of some basic facts.
2 Many countries .... (*derive*) their education system from what is valued in society in general.
3 How someone .... (*interpret*) a question will influence how they answer it.
4 It can be difficult when students move countries for their education to understand the .... (*proceed*) in the new education system.
5 He answered the question very .... (*specify*) and was awarded for doing so.

4 Match each set of words (1–5) to the words (a–e) to form collocations.

1 how many / costs / value
2 difficulty / problems / crisis
3 build to / manufacture to / meet
4 meet / fulfil / surplus to
5 foreign / economic / public

a policy
b estimate
c requirement
d specifications
e financial

5 Complete each of these sentences with a collocation from Exercise 4.

1 The countries' .... policy meant that taxes were often very high.
2 One problem many companies have is that they underestimate the .... of starting a business and so quickly build up high levels of debt.
3 The manager was no longer needed and was considered to be .... requirements.
4 Manufactured goods are required to .... specifications of safety standards in many countries.
5 Nearly all companies and economies have financial concerns that can easily be managed, but occasionally the situation can build to a financial .... and cause many companies to go bankrupt.

Sub-list 2

The words in these exercises all come from Sub-list 2 of the AWL.

1 Match the words (1–10) to their definitions (a–j).

1 affect
2 aspect
3 consequences
4 evaluation
5 impact
6 maintenance
7 obtain
8 participation
9 perceive
10 relevant

a one part of a situation, problem, etc.

b a judgement of the value or importance of something

c when you take part in something

d a powerful effect that someone or something has on a situation or person

e to come to an opinion about something or have a belief in it

f something that continues to exist

g connected with what is being discussed or happening

h to have an influence on someone or something

i to get something by asking, buying or working for it

j the results of an action or situation, which often negative

> 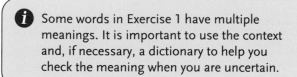 Some words in Exercise 1 have multiple meanings. It is important to use the context and, if necessary, a dictionary to help you check the meaning when you are uncertain.

2 Complete this table with the different forms of words from Exercise 1.

verb	noun	adjective	adverb
affect	effect	1	effectively
	consequence	consequent	2 ....
3	evaluation	evaluative	
4	impact		
5	maintenance		
obtain		6	
7	participation 8	participatory	
perceive	9		
	10	relevant	

3 Complete each of these sentences with the word in brackets in the correct form.

1 One role of a manager is to .... (*evaluate*) the performance of staff.

2 Modern management methods encourage the .... (*participate*) of staff in the decision-making process.

3 Some people try to .... (*obtain*) a senior post through qualifications, whereas others value experience.

4 The .... (*maintain*) of harmonious relationships between staff can be challenging, but at the same time a certain amount of conflict can lead to a creative environment.

5 The .... (*perceive*) of a manager as opposed to a leader is one that is more administrative.

6 The students are required to answer the question using only .... (*relevance*) information; they should not include anything that is irrelevant.

4 Match each set of words (1–4) to the words (a–d) to form collocations.

1 adversely / deeply
2 dire / disastrous / face the
3 major / significant / environmental
4 key / business / positive

a consequences
b impact
c affect
d aspect

5 Complete each of these sentences with a collocation from Exercise 4.

1 Whether the outcome is positive or negative, leaders often have to .... consequences of their decisions.

2 Many consumers now make a purchase by considering the .... impact of the product on the world.

3 Unexpectedly, the decision .... affected the company, causing a number of people to lose their jobs.

4 All aspects of the decision needed to be considered. It was not enough to consider only the .... aspect.

Sub-list 3

The words in these exercises all come from Sub-list 3 of the AWL.

1 Match the words (1–10) to their definitions (a–j).

1 component
2 constraint
3 deduction
4 illustrate
5 implys
6 justification
7 outcome
8 proportion
9 sufficient
10 validity

a to show the meaning, especially by using examples

b a good explanation or reason for something

c to state an idea without saying it directly

d the amount or number when compared with the whole

e something which controls something within particular limits

f enough

g something that can be accepted based on truth or reason

h when a decision or answer is reached based on what is known

i a result or effect of an action or situation

j a part which combines with other parts to create something bigger

> **i** Some words in Exercise 1 have multiple meanings. It is important to use the context and, if necessary, a dictionary to help you check the meaning when you are uncertain.

2 Complete this table with the different forms of words from Exercise 1.

verb	noun	adjective	adverb
1 _____	constraint	2 _____	
3 _____	deduction	deducible deductive	
illustrate	4 _____	illustrative	
imply	implication	5 _____	implicitly
6 _____	justification	justifiable	7 _____
	proportion	proportional proportionate	8 _____ proportionately
suffice	sufficiency	sufficient	9 _____
validate	10 _____ validity	valid	validly

3 Complete each of these sentences with the word in brackets in the correct form.

1 His approach was very _____ (deduce), using only the information and knowledge he had.

2 Without stating it directly, the teacher _____ (imply) that she was progressing well.

3 There was no _____ (justify) explanation for his behaviour.

4 Of all the languages in the world, speakers of English are _____ (proportion) higher than other languages.

5 The argument was not considered _____ (validate), as there was no evidence to support it.

4 Match each set of words (1–5) to the words (a–e) to form collocations.

1 financial / environmental / political
2 that / how
3 desirable / satisfactory / likely
4 basic / essential / individual
5 far from / barely / hardly

a illustrate
b outcome
c sufficient
d component
e constraint

5 Complete each of these sentences with a collocation from Exercise 4.

1 This example clearly illustrates _____ the company became successful.

2 The _____ outcome of poor motivation in language learning is of little progress being made.

3 Their performance was _____ sufficient and resulted in them failing.

4 The _____ components are not sufficient on their own and need to be implemented in conjunction with each other.

5 Many languages can disappear because of the _____ constraints placed on their use by a ruling or more powerful group.

Sub-list 4

The words in these exercises all come from Sub-list 4 of the AWL.

1 Match the words (1–10) to their definitions (a–j).

1 adequate	**a** yearly
2 annual	**b** relating to a person's own country
3 despite	**c** a national or racial group of
4 domestic	people
5 ethnic	**d** factors that limit how something
6 hence	can be done
7 promotion	**e** the reason or explanation for
8 parameters	something
9 prior	**f** enough for purpose
10 subsequent	**g** happening after something else
	h activities to advertise something
	i before
	j without taking notice of or being
	influenced by something

> ℹ️ Some words in Exercise 1 have multiple meanings. It is important to use the context and, if necessary, a dictionary to help you check the meaning when you are uncertain.

2 Complete this table with the different forms of words from Exercise 1.

verb	noun	adjective	adverb
	adequacy	adequate	1 ....
		annual	2 ....
domesticate	3	domestic domesticated	domestically
	4	ethnic	ethnically
5	promotion	6	
		subsequent	7 ....

3 Complete each of these sentences with the word in brackets in the correct form.

1 The consumption levels in some countries have been increasing .... (*annual*) for a number of years.

2 Each .... (*subsequent*) year has seen a rapid increase in world population for a number of decades now.

3 The .... (*domestic*) output of countries such as India and China continues to grow year on year.

4 India is one of the most .... (*ethnic*) diverse countries in the world.

5 A number of organizations are trying to .... (*promote*) the concept of consumers making sustainable changes to their lifestyles.

4 Complete each of the sentences below with one of the words from the box.

despite	hence	parameters	prior

1 .... having low incomes, many poor people in the developed world still have high levels of consumption.

2 The world is gradually running out of sources of fossil fuels, ... the drive to increase the development of renewable sources such as wind power.

3 .... to the opening of the Chinese economy, its consumption levels were relatively low.

4 There are strict .... limiting the development of nuclear energy in many countries.

5 Match each set of words (1–4) to the words (a–d) to form collocations.

1 market / economy / demand

2 background / minority / origin

3 heavily / indirectly / widely

4 prove to be / remain to be / seem to be

a adequate

b domestic

c ethnic

d promote

6 Complete each of these sentences with a collocation from Exercise 5.

1 Many health and government campaigns aimed at changing people's consumption patterns have not .... adequate, with consumption levels still at record levels.

2 Increases in GDP have also increased domestic .... of goods by Chinese consumers.

3 People who belong to an ethnic .... are often at most danger of losing their native language.

4 The success of an individual can .... promote other aspects of a country.

Sub-list 5

The words in these exercises all come from Sub-list 5 of the AWL.

1 Match the words (1–10) to their definitions (a–j).

1	adjustment	**a**	to cause something to exist
2	consultation	**b**	income received regularly
3	generate	**c**	a very small effect or amount
4	marginal	**d**	a small change
5	notion	**e**	to follow someone or something
6	pursue	**f**	compared with the fact; but
7	revenue	**g**	a discussion to obtain advice or opinions about something
8	stability		
9	substitution	**h**	when something is not likely to change or move
10	whereas	**i**	the use of a person or thing over another
		j	an idea or belief

> **i** Some words in Exercise 1 have multiple meanings. It is important to use the context and, if necessary, a dictionary to help you check the meaning when you are uncertain.

2 Complete this table with the different forms of words from Exercise 1.

verb	noun	adjective	adverb
1 _____	adjustment	adjustable	
2 _____	consultation 3 _____ consultancy	consultative	
marginalize	4 _____	marginal	marginally
pursue	5 _____	pursuant	
6 _____	7 _____ stability	stable	
8 _____	substitution		

3 Complete each of these sentences with the word in brackets in the correct form.

1 One challenge facing prisoners leaving prison is the _____ (*adjust*) to living back in society.

2 Governments use many _____ (*consult*) firms to help them develop policies.

3 Many criminals are considered to be _____ (*marginal*) in society.

4 Economic _____ (*stabilize*) often leads to a decrease in crime levels.

5 If one product is not available, many people _____ (*substitute*) it with a similar product.

4 Match each set of words (1–4) to the words (a–d) to form collocations.

1 revenue / profits / income

2 accept / challenge / reject

3 a goal / interest / a career

4 lost / tax / generate

a pursue

b generate

c revenue

d a notion

5 Complete each of these sentences with a collocation from Exercise 4.

1 When some people change jobs, they opt to pursue _____ in law.

2 Whilst turnover is important to a company, its main aim is to generate _____ .

3 Governments use _____ revenue to pay for services such as healthcare and education.

4 Many experts now _____ the notion that criminals are solely born, and it is more widely accepted that both genetics and environment play a role.

Sub-list 6

The words in these exercises all come from Sub-list 6 of the AWL.

1 Match the words (1–10) to their definitions (a–j).

1 cite
2 discrimination
3 enhance
4 explicit
5 incorporate
6 precede
7 presumption
8 rational
9 scope
10 trace

a to improve the quality or strength of something
b to come before
c to write or speak words from a particular text or writer
d believing something is true without proof
e treating someone differently to other people, usually negatively, because of their skin colour, sex, etc.
f showing clear thought or reason
g to include something as part of something larger
h the range covered by a book, discussion programme, etc.
i to find the origin of something
j clear and exact

 Some words in Exercise 1 have multiple meanings. It is important to use the context and, if necessary, a dictionary to help you check the meaning when you are uncertain.

2 Complete this table with the different forms of words from Exercise 1.

verb	noun	adjective	adverb
cite	1		
2	discrimination	discriminating	
3	enhancement	enhanced	
		explicit	4 ....
incorporate	5		
precede	6 .... precedence		
7	presumption	presumptuous presumable	presumptuously presumably
rationalize	rationalization	8	9 ....
trace	trace	10	

3 Complete each of these sentences with the word in brackets in the correct form.

1 It is vital to .... (*cite*) correctly any source used in writing.
2 Selecting the right people for a team can .... (*enhance*) the performance of the group.
3 .... (*precede*) must be given to protecting jobs.
4 .... (*presume*) the statement is correct, but it does lack proof.
5 The decision to cut staff by 10% was seen as tough, but given the circumstances, it was probably .... (*rationalize*).

4 Match each set of words (1–5) to the words (a–e) to form collocations.

1 beyond the / narrow the / limited
2 age / gender / positive
3 highly / quite / increasingly
4 in / into / within
5 attempt to / help to / fail to

a explicit
b scope
c incorporate
d trace
e discrimination

5 Complete each of these sentences with a collocation from Exercise 4.

1 The outcome became .... explicit as more and more information was uncovered.
2 Many research proposals are too broad, and students often have to .... scope of the proposal.
3 The idea was so good it was quickly incorporated .... the plan.
4 Despite much research, they .... trace the origin of the product.
5 To help reduce .... discrimination, many countries around the world have removed compulsory retirement, meaning people can work as long as they desire.

Sub-list 7

The words in these exercises all come from Sub-list 7 of the AWL.

1 Match the words (1–10) to their definitions (a–j).

1 advocate	**a** to publicly support something
2 eliminate	**b** to form an opinion or guess something is true based on something you know
3 empirical	
4 foundation	
5 infer	**c** something that exists and is often interesting or unusual
6 isolate	**d** to take away or remove
7 phenomenon	**e** something that is important that is dealt with before other things
8 priority	
9 successive	**f** to separate or keep separate one thing from others
10 ultimately	**g** happening one after the other without break
	h based on experience or observation, not theory
	i finally, after a series of things have happened
	j when something is established

> Some words in Exercise 1 have multiple meanings. It is important to use the context and, if necessary, a dictionary to help you check the meaning when you are uncertain.

2 Complete this table with the different forms of words from Exercise 1.

verb	noun	adjective	adverb
advocate	1 .... advocacy		
eliminate	2		
		empirical	3 ....
infer	4	inferred	
5	isolation	isolated	
	phenomenon	6	phenomenally
7	priority 8		
succeed	successor 9	successive	successively
		10	ultimately

3 Complete each of these sentences with the word in brackets in the correct form.

1 Although it was not stated explicitly, it was easy to .... (*infer*) what was meant.

2 .... (*isolate*) from other languages can allow a small language to survive much longer than one that is near dominant languages.

3 Many countries of the world have made English a .... (*prioritize*) language in their education system.

4 To judge a student's level, placement tests often become .... (*succeed*) more difficult the further a student gets through the test.

5 .... (*ultimate*), most people study in order to get a better job.

4 Match each set of words (1–4) to the words (a–d) to form collocations.

1 enthusiastic / strong / main

2 solid / economic / undermine the

3 seek to / designed to / impossible to

4 widespread / new / political

a advocate

b eliminate

c phenomenon

d foundation

5 Complete each of these sentences with a collocation from Exercise 4.

1 Lombroso was one of the .... advocates of biological links to the causes of crime.

2 Despite much effort, it has proven .... eliminate unethical behaviour from many companies and cultures.

3 The Internet was originally a military tool, but in the 1990s, it became a .... phenomenon, quickly spreading throughout the world.

4 The company was fortunate in that much investment gave it a strong .... foundation on which to base its growth.

6 What is the meaning of *empirical evidence*? Why do you think it is considered so important?

Sub-list 8

The words in these exercises all come from Sub-list 8 of the AWL.

1 Match the words (1–10) to their definitions (a–j).

1 accumulation
2 contradiction
3 denote
4 deviation
5 eventually
6 exhibit
7 implicit
8 inevitably
9 predominantly
10 thereby

a to represent something
b something that is different from the normal way of behaving
c to show something publicly
d in a way that cannot be avoided
e an amount of something that has been collected
f mainly
g as a result of this action
h when something is so different from something else that one of them must be wrong
i suggested but not directly communicated
j in the end, especially after a lot of effort or problems

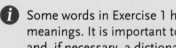 Some words in Exercise 1 have multiple meanings. It is important to use the context and, if necessary, a dictionary to help you check the meaning when you are uncertain.

2 Complete this table with the different forms of words from Exercise 1.

verb	noun	adjective	adverb
1	accumulation		
contradict	contradiction	2	
denote	3		
4	deviation		
	eventuality	5	eventually
exhibit	6 .... exhibitor		
implicate imply	implication	implicit	7 ....
	inevitability	8	inevitably
predominate	9	10	predominantly

3 Complete each of these sentences with the word in brackets in the correct form.

1 The colour green .... (*denote*) envy in many countries, but in America, it represents money.
2 His motivation .... (*eventuality*) led to him becoming a successful language learner.
3 One mistake many small businesses make is that they believe success is .... (*inevitability*).
4 The rapid growth in obesity .... (*predominate*) stems from changes to modern diets and lifestyles.
5 Negative personality traits .... (*exhibit*) in team work can lead to the breakdown of the group.

4 Match each set of words (1–4) to the words (a–d) to form collocations.

1 slowly / steadily / rapidly
2 clearly / completely / directly
3 by / from
4 criticism / threat / assumption

a deviate
b accumulate
c implicit
d contradict

5 Complete each of these sentences with a collocation from Exercise 4.

1 The essay deviated .... the topic too far, and as a result received a low mark for relevance.
2 In times of economic growth, it can be much easier to .... accumulate wealth.
3 This paragraph states arguments that .... contradict those in the previous one. They are the exact opposite.
4 Her comments were seen as an implicit .... of the company.

Sub-list 9

The words in these exercises all come from Sub-list 9 of the AWL.

1 Match the words (1–10) to their definitions (a–j).

1	anticipate	a	a promise
2	assurance	b	to start
3	attain	c	to succeed in getting something
4	coincide	d	a disagreement about something that usually affects a lot of people
5	commence		
6	controversy e	e	to reduce in size or importance
7	devote	f	important as part of a whole
8	diminish	g	a situation or event that causes something, usually bad, to start
9	integral	h	to happen near or at the same time
10	trigger	i	to give all your effort and time to something or someone
		j	to imagine or expect something to happen

 Some words in Exercise 1 have multiple meanings. It is important to use the context and, if necessary, a dictionary to help you check the meaning when you are uncertain.

2 Complete this table with the different forms of words from Exercise 1.

verb	noun	adjective	adverb
anticipate	1	anticipatory	
2	assurance	assured	assuredly
attain	attainment	3	
coincide	4	coincidental	5 ....
commence	6		
	controversy	controversial	7 ....
devote	8 .... devotee	devoted	devotedly
integrate	integration	integral	9 ....
trigger	10		

3 Complete each of these sentences with the word in brackets in the correct form.

1 The launch of the product caused much .... (*anticipate*), from both customers and industry experts.

2 With hard work, high levels of fluency are .... (*attain*).

3 Although the two products were similar, it was seen as .... (*coincide*), and nobody believed one had copied the other.

4 The .... (*commence*) of trade agreements with another country can lead to rapid growth in a country's economy.

4 Match each set of words (1–5) to the words (a–e) to form collocations.

1 despite / written / formal
2 prove / highly / politically
3 entirely / specifically / mainly
4 part / to
5 a response / a memory

a controversial
b integral
c assurance
d trigger
e devote

5 Complete each of these sentences with a collocation from Exercise 4.

1 Bribery is seen as .... controversial in some countries, but as a way of life in others.

2 Education is seen as an integral .... of changing people's behaviour.

3 .... assurances that the deal was entirely legal, many people were suspicious that corruption had played a part in it.

4 Advertising tries primarily to trigger .... in a consumer that results in their desire to purchase the product or service.

5 They were asked to .... devote more time to the development of ideas and not to other areas of the presentation.

Sub-list 10

The words in these exercises all come from Sub-list 10 of the AWL.

1 Match the words (1–10) to their definitions (a–j).

1	collapse	**a**	to fall down, to fail
2	compile	**b**	to put information from different places together in a book or report
3	conceive		
4	convince	**c**	in the same way
5	invoke	**d**	not willing to do something
6	likewise	**e**	despite what has just been done or said
7	nonetheless		
8	persistent	**f**	to imagine something
9	reluctant	**g**	difficult to get rid of or lasting a long time
10	whereby		
		h	to make someone have a particular feeling or remember something
		i	by which method or way
		j	to persuade

 Some words in Exercise 1 have multiple meanings. It is important to use the context and, if necessary, a dictionary to help you check the meaning when you are uncertain.

2 Complete this table with the different forms of words from Exercise 1.

verb	noun	adjective	adverb
collapse	1	collapsible	
compile	2	compiled	
conceive	conception	3	conceivably
convince		convincing	4 ....
5	6	persistent	persistently
	7	reluctant	8 ....

3 Complete each of the sentences below with a word from the box.

invokes	likewise	nonetheless	whereby

1 They have set up a plan .... employees are selected by personality above and beyond other criteria.

2 Age is influential in consumer behaviour; .... , so is gender.

3 Laws are in place to reduce corruption; .... , it is widely practised throughout the world.

4 The word leader .... images of great people who have inspired many others.

4 Match each set of words (1–6) to the words (a–f) to form collocations.

1 close to / sudden / economic

2 from / for

3 popular / general / original

4 firmly / by no means / fully

5 in / with

6 deep / growing / understandable

a compile

b convinced

c conception

d persist

e collapse

f reluctance

5 Complete each of these sentences with a collocation from Exercise 4.

1 A list of sources needs to be compiled .... a bibliography.

2 Whilst I can see the logic, I am .... convinced it is the right plan.

3 The .... conception of the product was nothing like the final product in reality.

4 Even though educating people about healthy eating appears to be failing, the government continues to persist .... this approach.

5 The company appears to be .... collapse.

6 There was an .... reluctance to invest a lot of money into the research, as it was untried area. However, it was also a vital area that many know needs to be investigated.

Academic Word List

Sub-list 1

This sub-list contains the most frequent words of the Academic Word List in the Academic Corpus.

analysis	definition	indicate	procedure
approach	derived	individual	process
area	distribution	interpretation	required
assessment	economic	involved	research
assume	environment	issues	response
authority	established	labour	role
available	estimate	legal	section
benefit	evidence	legislation	sector
concept	export	major	significant
consistent	factors	method	similar
constitutional	financial	occur	source
context	formula	percent	specific
contract	function	period	structure
create	identified	policy	theory
data	income	principle	variable

Sub-list 2

This sub-list contains the second most frequent words in the Academic Word List from the Academic Corpus.

achieve	consequences	institute	region
acquisition	construction	investment	regulations
administration	consumer	items	relevant
affect	credit	journal	resident
appropriate	cultural	maintenance	resources
aspects	design	normal	restricted
assistance	distinction	obtained	security
categories	elements	participation	sought
chapter	equation	perceived	select
commission	evaluation	positive	site
community	features	potential	strategies
complex	final	previous	survey
computer	focus	primary	text
conclusion	impact	purchase	traditional
conduct	injury	range	transfer

Sub-list 3

This sub-list contains the third most frequent words of the Academic Word List in the Academic Corpus.

alternative	criteria	interaction	registered
circumstances	deduction	justification	reliance
comments	demonstrate	layer	removed
compensation	document	link	scheme
components	dominant	location	sequence
consent	emphasis	maximum	sex
considerable	ensure	minorities	shift
constant	excluded	negative	specified
constraints	framework	outcomes	sufficient
contribution	funds	partnership	task
convention	illustrated	philosophy	technical
coordination	immigration	physical	techniques
core	implies	proportion	technology
corporate	initial	published	validity
corresponding	instance	reaction	volume

Sub-list 4

This sub-list contains the fourth most frequent words of the Academic Word List in the Academic Corpus.

access	debate	internal	prior
adequate	despite	investigation	professional
annual	dimensions	job	project
apparent	domestic	label	promote
approximated	emerged	mechanism	regime
attitudes	error	obvious	resolution
attributed	ethnic	occupational	retained
civil	goals	option	series
code	granted	output	statistics
commitment	hence	overall	status
communication	hypothesis	parallel	stress
concentration	implementation	parameters	subsequent
conference	implications	phase	sum
contrast	imposed	predicted	summary
cycle	integration	principal	undertaken

Sub-list 5

This sub-list contains the fifth most frequent words of the Academic Word List in the Academic Corpus.

academic	enable	licence	pursue
adjustment	energy	logic	ratio
alter	enforcement	marginal	rejected
amendment	entities	medical	revenue
aware	equivalent	mental	stability
capacity	evolution	modified	styles
challenge	expansion	monitoring	substitution
clause	exposure	network	sustainable
compounds	external	notion	symbolic
conflict	facilitate	objective	target
consultation	fundamental	orientation	transition
contact	generated	perspective	trend
decline	generation	precise	version
discretion	image	prime	welfare
draft	liberal	psychology	whereas

Sub-list 6

This sub-list contains the sixth most frequent words of the Academic Word List in the Academic Corpus.

abstract	diversity	incidence	nevertheless
accurate	domain	incorporated	overseas
acknowledged	edition	index	preceding
aggregate	enhanced	inhibition	presumption
allocation	estate	initiatives	rational
assigned	exceed	input	recovery
attached	expert	instructions	revealed
author	explicit	intelligence	scope
bond	federal	interval	subsidiary
brief	fees	lecture	tapes
capable	flexibility	migration	trace
cited	furthermore	minimum	transformation
cooperative	gender	ministry	transport
discrimination	ignored	motivation	underlying
display	incentive	neutral	utility

Sub-list 7

This sub-list contains the seventh most frequent words of the Academic Word List in the Academic Corpus.

adaptation	deny	identical	release
adults	differentiation	ideology	reverse
advocate	disposal	inferred	simulation
aid	dynamic	innovation	solely
channel	eliminate	insert	somewhat
chemical	empirical	intervention	submitted
classical	equipment	isolated	successive
comprehensive	extract	media	survive
comprise	file	mode	thesis
confirmed	finite	paradigm	topic
contrary	foundation	phenomenon	transmission
converted	global	priority	ultimately
couple	grade	prohibited	unique
decades	guarantee	publication	visible
definite	hierarchical	quotation	voluntary

Sub-list 8

This sub-list contains the eighth most frequent words of the Academic Word List in the Academic Corpus.

abandon	contradiction	induced	random
accompanied	crucial	inevitably	reinforced
accumulation	currency	infrastructure	restore
ambiguous	denote	inspection	revision
appendix	detected	intensity	schedule
appreciation	deviation	manipulation	tension
arbitrary	displacement	minimised	termination
automatically	dramatic	nuclear	theme
bias	eventually	offset	thereby
chart	exhibit	paragraph	uniform
clarity	exploitation	plus	vehicle
conformity	fluctuations	practitioners	via
commodity	guidelines	predominantly	virtually
complement	highlighted	prospect	widespread
contemporary	implicit	radical	visual

Sub-list 9

This sub-list contains the ninth most frequent words of the Academic Word List in the Academic Corpus.

accommodation	conversely	mature	restraints
analogous	device	mediation	revolution
anticipated	devoted	medium	rigid
assurance	diminished	military	route
attained	distortion	minimal	scenario
behalf	duration	mutual	sphere
bulk	erosion	norms	subordinate
ceases	ethical	overlap	supplementary
coherence	format	passive	suspended
coincide	founded	portion	team
commenced	inherent	preliminary	temporary
incompatible	insights	protocol	trigger
concurrent	integral	qualitative	unified
confined	intermediate	refine	violation
controversy	manual	relaxed	vision

Sub-list 10

This sub-list contains the least frequent words of the Academic Word List in the Academic Corpus.

adjacent	depression	levy	posed
albeit	encountered	likewise	reluctant
assembly	enormous	nonetheless	so called
collapse	forthcoming	notwithstanding	straightforward
colleagues	inclination	odd	undergo
compiled	integrity	ongoing	whereby
conceived	intrinsic	panel	
convinced	invoked	persistent	

Writing checklist

The following checklist can be used to review your work before you hand it in. Check each area carefully and be honest in your evaluation.

	Yes	No
Essay structure and organization		
Does my introduction get the reader's interest?	☐	☐
If it is an opinion-based essay, is there a clear line of argument in my thesis?	☐	☐
Does each paragraph have a clear topic?	☐	☐
Is everything related to the main topic of each paragraph?	☐	☐
Are the paragraphs logically ordered?	☐	☐
Does the conclusion restate the main argument?	☐	☐
Does the conclusion summarize the main ideas well?	☐	☐
Using sources		
Have I referenced all ideas I have included from other sources?	☐	☐
Have I used the correct method for direct and indirect referencing?	☐	☐
For indirect references, have I used my own words to express the idea but made sure the meaning stays the same?	☐	☐
Have I introduced and commented on the references I've used?	☐	☐
Have I included a bibliography using the correct method?	☐	☐
Critical thinking		
Have I chosen reliable sources for my essay?	☐	☐
Have I questioned who wrote the information in terms of reliability, bias and expertise?	☐	☐
Are the arguments logical?	☐	☐
Have I questioned (and not simply accepted) the ideas of others?	☐	☐
Language focus		
Is my language suitably academic?	☐	☐
Have I checked the spelling?	☐	☐
Have I checked the accuracy of grammar, vocabulary and form?	☐	☐
Have I used the correct linking language?	☐	☐

Feedback checklist

It is important that any feedback you receive should be fed into future writing. Use this form to help you keep a record of issues you need to think about for future assessments.

What comments or corrections were made on my essay's structure and organization?

What comments were made about my use of sources?

What comments were made about my arguments or evaluation of sources I used?

What were the main language errors that were highlighted?

Are there any other comments I need to pay particular attention to?